Dying Unto Life

Dying Unto Life

Arthur C. McGill on
New God, New Death, New Life

Theological Fascinations

Volume Two

EDITED BY
DAVID CAIN

CASCADE *Books* · Eugene, Oregon

DYING UNTO LIFE
Arthur C. McGill on New God, New Death, New Life

Theological Fascinations

Cascade Books
An Imprint of Wipf and Stock Publishers
199 W. 8th Ave., Suite 3
Eugene, OR 97401

www.wipfandstock.com

ISBN 13: 978-1-60899-151-8

Cataloging-in-Publication data:

McGill, Arthur C.

    Dying unto life : Arthur C. McGill on new God, new death, new life / Arthur C. McGill.

    xvi + 154 p. ; 23 cm. —Includes bibliographical references.

    Theological Fascinations

    ISBN 13: 978-1-60899-151-8

    1. Death—Religious aspects—Christianity. 2. Death—Social aspects—United States. 3. Jesus Christ—Person and offices. I. Title. II. Series.

BT 825 M19 2013

Manufactured in the USA.

For Arthur McGill and Lucy McGill

For Bill May and Paul Ramsey

For Chuck Balestri and Egbert Leigh
and in memory of Diane and Lizzie, their wonderful wives

For my wife Marlyne, our daughters Sarah Marlyne and Kristin Lise,
and our sons-in-law Eddie Lee Naylor and Seamus Michael Geary

With proud, loving welcomes to grandsons

Conor Michael Geary
born 8 September, 2009

Noah Cain Naylor
born 20 March, 2011

In gratitude.

The cross was the place of decisive engagement between God and our negative destructive vitality. It was therefore the place of decisive victory–of victory not for death but for God and for life.

This is the center of the Christian religion. This gives direction to the whole Christian life. It must be grasped carefully and delicately.

—ARTHUR C. MCGILL, "DYING UNTO LIFE: A NEW KIND OF ALIVENESS"

Contents

Foreword ix
C. FitzSimons Allison

Acknowledgments xiii

Introduction—Arthur C. McGill: A Theological Memoir 1
David Cain

I. Inverted Values: Death as Occasion for Nourishment Anew 23

II. The Positive Meaning of Need: Revolutionary Gratitude 33

III. Identity and Death: The Human Condition in Jesus 46

IV. An Alien Good: End of the Known 74

V. Dying Unto Life: A New Kind of Aliveness 79

VI. Death in Baptism and Eucharist: Identity by Having or by Expending 103

VII. Satanic or Christic God: God Does Not Stomp on Satan 123

VIII. Theological Fragments 142

Appendix 151

Foreword

The present conflicts between conservative tradition and liberal accommodation to the age are approached by Arthur McGill in profound and startling reversals of conventional wisdom. Beginning with death, he shows that popular understanding of death seriously distorts Christian teaching. Death is not outside of us, external to us. Rather, it is an intrinsic part of human nature. In a certain sense it is natural. We not only die by death but we live by it. Everything we eat had first to die and none of us is going to get out of this world alive.

The culture's assumption that death is something that comes to us from outside ourselves is not only misleading but it obscures from us the fact that it is love, not death, that comes from without ourselves. The world teaches us to hope that our needs will be met, and, as a result, we will no longer need. We can then become independent. McGill's surprising reversal shows that Christian love does not replace need or neediness but renders us all more needy and dependent on God.

The world's understanding of gift is that gifts satisfy needs, whereas the gift of divine love, forgiveness, and justification opens up more vulnerability and an increasingly dependent need for God's love. Here our needs are not lessened but made more apparent. Many voices have told us that gratitude is the indispensable necessity for joy but not how we are enabled to be grateful. McGill, on the other hand, shows us the source of our gratitude. Only by recognizing our neediness can we be truly grateful ("They that are whole need not a physician" [Matt 9:12]). Otherwise gratitude is not grace but mere duty that only increases our guilt. It is our need that unites us with God. The clarity for this claim comes from the many biblical texts showing Jesus' utter and continuing dependence upon the Father (John 14:28, 31; Luke 22:42).

These so-called subordination texts have been used by Arian heretics in all periods of history and they thereby miss the gracious trinitarian teaching that Christian subordination is not inequality. Christian slaves, servants, secretaries, soldiers have not lost dignity by being in subordinate rolls.

Would that historians of the creeds and councils would approach their subjects with a pastoral depth that would free the teaching of the Trinity and Christology from its academic and pedantic closet. What is at stake, according to McGill, is the very identity of human beings. Identity gained by what we have, what we possess, underscored by human nature's drive to independence, is a satanic religion. McGill tells us that each person who seeks "to be real by securing something for himself and not expending himself for and into others thereby declares that the ruler of reality is also one who secures and holds things for himself, who possesses and does not share. The New Testament name for God when seen in this way is Satan."

To approach this intractable human dilemma of selfishness on a merely ethical level is completely futile. In a world striving for identity by possessions, by seeking and having independence (Ayn Rand's world) it would be foolish or even insane to act unselfishly. With these assumptions of the world it is foolish to ask such persons for unselfishness for, as McGill shows, it is not in their power to choose.

As with scholarly treatments of the Trinity and Christology, the world of academic soteriology would be greatly refreshed by McGill's explanation of "ecstatic identity." We cannot advance until we relinquish a moralistic conception of evil. Human nature has been given what it could not accomplish: an identity outside its self's center, an ecstatic identity. This gift is Jesus Christ, who is himself the love that frees us from our self as center.

This love is a power radically different from the world's power. A possible title for this work was *God Does Not Stomp on Satan*, one of McGill's inimical observations. This sentence points to the words of Jesus to his disciples in the Garden of Gethsemane: "Do you think that I cannot appeal to my Father, and he will at once send me more than twelve legions of angels?" (Matt 26:53) and "My kingship is not of this world; if it were of this world, my servants would fight . . ." (John 18:36). In this light Easter is not merely a fact that God is more powerful than Satan, or that he imposes his will on Satan, but that Satan is undermined by a deeper and different power of love. This understanding of love's power is judgment on us all as we rely on modern legions to coerce, impose, and dominate evil powers. McGill warns that when the name of Jesus is invoked for dominating power the power of Jesus is withdrawn.

Arthur McGill's sometimes surprising but always invaluable teachings involving unexpected depths have been revealed by an heroic endeavor of careful investigation, interpretation of notes and deciphering handwriting by the editor. We are especially indebted to David Cain for this diligence but even more for the devotion and high regard he had for his teacher. This work has a life and passion that would have been inaccessible without this devotion. (Yet it in no way lessened Cain's ability to disagree with McGill in such matters as the latter's view of positions taken by Paul Ramsey.) We have in this work a remarkable example of diligent editorial care that discloses the masterful theology of Arthur McGill, a witness of unashamed and profound Christian faith.

C. FitzSimons Allison, DPhil (Oxon.)
Bishop of South Carolina, Retired

Acknowledgments

Grateful acknowledgments are here given to the following for permission to quote from copyrighted works. An attempt has been made to identify and to obtain permission from all relevant parties. Thanks to Ms. Paula Bettencourt of Copyright Clearance Center, Danvers, Massachusetts, for her assistance with permissions. Where material is quoted and no acknowledgment is given the editor has been advised that permission is not required.

Thanks to Ms. Sherri Feldman, Ms. Deborah Foley, and Random House, Inc. for permission to quote from W. H. Auden's poem, "In Time of War," in W. H. Auden, *Collected Poems of W. H. Auden*, © 1976 by Edward Mendelson, William Meredith and Monroe K. Speaks, Executors of the Estate of W. H. Auden. Used by permission of Random House, Inc.

Thanks to Ms. Patricia Lo, Augustinian Heritage Institute, for permission to quote from St. Augustine, *Sermons III (51–94) on the New Testament*, New City Press, 1991.

Thanks to Mr. Jim Wagner and Continuum International Publishing Group for permission to quote from Karl Barth, *Church Dogmatics*, The Doctrine of Reconciliation, IV, I, T. & T. Clark, 1956.

Thanks to Ms. Barbara D. Porter and Abingdon Press / Cokesbury for permission to quote from Simon Cohen, "Bashan" in *Interpreter's Dictionary of the Bible*, vol. 1, ed. George Arthur Buttrick, Abingdon Press, 1962, and to quote from Leander Keck, "New Testament Views of Death" in *Perspectives on Death*, Liston O. Mills, ed., Abingdon Press, 1969. Used by permission.

Thanks Random House, Inc. for permission to quote from James Dickey's poem, "The Eye-Beaters," James Dickey, *The Eye-Beaters, Blood, Victory, Madness, Buckhead*, © 1968, 1969, 1970 by James Dickey. Used by permission of Doubleday, a division of Random House, Inc.

Acknowledgments

Thanks to Ms. Joy Azmitia, Ms. Maryann Yin and Russell and Volkening, Inc. for permission to publish Kenneth Fearing's poem, "American Rhapsody (4)," *Collected Poems of Kenneth Fearing*, Random House, 1940.

Thanks to Ms. Jennifer Chang Rowley, Ms. Bette Graber, Ms. Minwattie Sawh and Random House, Inc. for permission to quote from Dag Hammarskjöld, *Markings*, trans. by W. H. Auden and Leif Sjöberg © 1964, copyright renewed 1992 by Alfred A. Knopf, a division of Random House, Inc., and Faber & Faber Ltd. Used by permission of Alfred A. Knopf, a division of Random House, Inc. Thanks for permission to quote John Updike's poem, "Seven Stanzas at Easter," John Updike, *Collected Poems 1953–1993*, © 1993 by John Updike. Used by permission of Alfred A. Knopf, a division of Random House, Inc.

Thanks to Ms. Sharon Swados and HarperCollins Publishers for permission to reference Martin Heidegger, *Being and Time*, 1962.

Thanks to Mr. Tom DeVries and Wm. B. Eerdmans Publishing Co. for permission to quote from Eberhard Jüngel, *God as the Mystery of the World*, 1983, and Alan E. Lewis, *Between Cross and Resurrection*, 2001.

Thanks to Penguin Group (USA), Inc. for permission to quote from John Keats, "Ode to a Nightingale" in *Romantic Poets: Blake to Poe*, eds. W. H. Auden and Norman Holmes Pearson, The Viking Press, 1950, and thanks to Ms. Blanche Brown and Penguin Group for permission to publish D. H. Lawrence's poem, "We Are Transmitters," D. H. Lawrence, *The Complete Poems of D. H. Lawrence*, ed. V. de Sola Pinto and F. W. Roberts, © 1964, 1971 by Angelo Ravagli and C. M. Weekley, Executors of the Estate of Frieda Lawrence Ravagli. Used by permission of Viking Penguin, a division of Penguin Group (USA) Inc.

Thanks to Ms. Laura E. Anderson and Beacon Press for permission to quote from Herbert Marcuse, *Eros and Civilization*, Beacon Press, 1955.

Thanks to Ms. Velma Felix and McGraw-Hill Companies for permission to quote from Herbert Marcuse, "The Ideology of Death" in Herman Feifel, ed., *The Meaning of Death*, 1959.

Thanks to Ms. Florence B. Eichin and Mr. Jeffrey Corrick, Penguin Group (USA), Inc. for permission to quote from Friedrich Nietzsche's "The Night Song," *Thus Spoke Zarathustra*, in *The Portable Nietzsche*, trans. Walter Kaufmann, The Viking Press, 1954.

Thanks to Ms. Claudia Acevedo and Princeton University Press for permission to quote from *Ancient Near Eastern Tests Relating to the Old Testament*, ed. James B. Pritchard, © Princeton University Press, 1950.

Thanks to Ms. Joyce A. Griffin and The Hastings Center for permission to quote from Paul Ramsey, "The Indignity of 'Death with Dignity,'" *Hastings Center Studies*, 1974.

Thanks to Ms. Sarah Williams and Ed Victor Ltd. for permission to publish Stephen Spender's poem, "What I Expected," *Collected Poems: 1928–1953*, Random House, 1934, and in *New Collected Poems*, Stephen Spender, © 2004. Reprinted by kind permission of the Estate of Stephen Spender.

Thanks to Ms. Samantha Shea, Ms. Valerie Borchardt and Georges Borchardt, Inc. for permission to quote from Pierre Teilhard de Chardin, *Hymn of the Universe*, © 1961 by Editions du Seuil, English trans. © 1965 by William Collins Sons & Co., Ltd., London, and Harper & Row, Inc., New York. Reprinted by permission of Georges Borchardt, Inc., for Editions du Seuil.

Thanks to Ms. Christy Korrow and The Crossroad Publishing Company, Inc. for permission to quote from John E. Thiel, *God, Evil, and Innocent Suffering*, The Crossroad Publishing Company, 2002.

Thanks to Ms. Ruth Wantling for permission to publish William Wantling's poem, "Just Lately," *The Source*, Dust Book, 1966.

Thanks to Ms. Patricia Zline and The Rowman & Littlefield Publishing Group for permission to quote from Avery D. Weisman, *The Realization of Death*, Jason Aronson, Inc., 1974.

Thanks to Mr. Will Parkes and Darton, Longman & Todd for permission to quote from Rowan Williams, *Resurrection*, Darton, Longman & Todd, 1982.

◆

Introduction

Arthur C. McGill: A Theological Memoir[1]

DAVID CAIN

When on any occasion his father engaged in an argument with somebody . . . [Johannes Climacus] was all ears. . . . His father always allowed his opponent to state his whole case, and then would ask him very carefully whether he had anything more to say before he began his reply. . . . The father's rejoinder would follow, and lo! In a thrice everything would be changed. How this happened remained a riddle to J. C. But his soul was delighted by such a drama. The opponent would speak again, and J. C. would be still more attentive, so that he should miss nothing. . . . [T]he father . . . would then perorate, and J. C. could almost hear his heart beat, so impatiently did he await what should happen.

It did happen! In a twinkling everything would be inverted.[2]

---

1. This is a revision of a paper first presented at the American Academy of Religion, Southeastern Regional Annual Meeting, Atlanta, Georgia, 19 March, 1983, and originally published as "Arthur McGill: A Memoir" in *Harvard Theological Review*, 77:1 (1984) 95–111. I thank *Harvard Theological Review* for permission to republish the essay. The essay was written from the published works of Arthur McGill before I received from Lucy McGill boxes and boxes of file folders (474 in all plus several notebooks). Rarely did I draw on other materials available to me in mimeographed form, etc. Notable exceptions are "The Power of God and the Problem of Suffering" (see n. 13 below) and the "Identity and Death" paper, which becomes Chapter III in this volume and which I reference. Question: to revise and reference the article incorporating "new" materials or to let the original stand? I have taken the easy way out—to leave the original alone. Could the easy way also be the best, allowing sparks to jump from a reading of published works to "new" materials, contradicting, confirming—or both—the first reading and therein illuminating McGill's thought?

2. Søren Kierkegaard, *Johannes Climacus Or, De Omnibus Dubitandum Est*, trans. T. H. Croxall (Stanford: Stanford University Press, 1958), 107.

Perhaps these words of Søren Kierkegaard concerning young Johannes and his dialectical father are autobiographical. Perhaps they give us insight into one aspect of the relationship between young Søren and his father, Michael Pedersen Kierkegaard. I trust I do not write solely autobiographically when I apply them to the pedagogical power of Arthur Chute McGill.

Power—surely not the first word to suggest itself upon initially encountering McGill, a small man with something of the demeanor of a genial gargoyle. But maybe the last word. In any case, the *right* word to describe the concern of his thought—and to describe the substance of the man.

It was an inviting spring afternoon in 1962. A Princeton precept was convening—congealing—crowding into a little room at 48 University Place. McGill related to his students across a distance of polite formality. His students were "gentlemen"—this was before coeducation came to Princeton. Someone said something—something obvious, something fuzzy, something beside the point, or perhaps something insightful. McGill leaned back to receive and forward to respond, bringing his hands together, touching the tips of his fingers with eager, accelerating energy. "Y-e-e-s, isn't that interesting . . ." he began; and "It did happen! In a twinkling everything would be inverted." We were off on an extravaganza of ideas in motion, both dazzled and grasped, wondering what view was going to triumph—and how.

Part of McGill's power came from his inclination—a theologically informed inclination—to a theology of confrontation. I am thinking, for instance, of Jacques Ellul's autobiographical remark:

> I have sought *to confront* theological and biblical knowledge and sociological analysis *without trying to come to any artificial or philosophical synthesis*; instead, I try *to place the two face to face*, in order to shed some light on what is real socially and real spiritually.[3]

In the same way, McGill did not aim for easy correlation or synthesis. He guarded against "volatilizing" concepts (Kierkegaard's language) or cushioning collisions. Rather, if the collisions are there, let them be addressed and even intensified.

For example, when considering the presence of Christian theology within the university, McGill writes, "Irenic claims that . . . conflict

---

3. James Y. Holloway, ed., *Introducing Jacques Ellul* (Grand Rapids: Eerdmans, 1970), 6. Italics added. Jacques Ellul (1912–1994) was a brilliant and prolific French philosopher, sociologist, Christian theologian, and professor of law at the University of Bordeaux.

is unnecessary, that Christian theology and a faculty devoted to scholarship really share a common ground or pursue a common belief in reason, are simply false."[4] McGill seeks to uncover the bases of what he deems essential conflict in his doctoral dissertation entitled *The Place of Dogmatic Theology in the University*.[5] He completed it at about age thirty-four; it is a work of maturity and begins characteristically with McGill stacking the deck against dogmatic theology in the university. On the side of dogmatic theology, he chooses to work with Karl Barth because, he says, "here many of the problems are posed in their most extreme form";[6] and that is exactly what McGill wants.

For McGill, good theology and good poetry can come by way of some of the same sensitivities. Appreciation of literary form is evidenced in his work. In the dissertation, he emphasizes "the poetic style of the actual fragments" of the early Greek thinkers, and writes:

> As long as human thinking is seen as the search for clear and distinct ideas about objective reality, the task of reporting the content of a philosophy consists simply in repeating the several ideas it contains in a clear way. The question of a philosopher's literary form and style, the particular way he juxtaposes his ideas within sentences, his vagueness at one point in comparison with his clarity at another—all these considerations do not come into play.[7]

The point is, of course, that they *should* come into play, that they are inextricably related to the content of the thought.

There is an analogy between McGill's treatment of poetry in relation to Christian faith and his characterization of the Christian life as one of

---

4. Arthur C. McGill, "The Ambiguous Position of Christian Theology" in Paul Ramsey and John F. Wilson, eds., *The Study of Religion in Colleges and Universities* (Princeton: Princeton University Press, 1970), 123. This volume resulted from a conference held at Princeton University in the spring of 1968 honoring George Finger Thomas on the occasion of his retirement. George Thomas (1899–1977) was the founding chair of Princeton's Department of Religion in 1947. A "Memorial Resolution" submitted by R. Paul Ramsey, Malcolm L. Diamond, John F. Wilson, and Philip H. Ashby reads in part: "In many respects George Thomas' career as a teacher-scholar was central in the history of the establishment and development of the academic study of religion in higher education in the United States in the middle decades of the twentieth century."

5. Arthur C. McGill, *The Place of Dogmatic Theology in the University* (PhD diss., Yale University, 1961).

6. Ibid., 11. Karl Barth (1886–1968), the great Swiss theologian, is a major voice in Christian theology.

7. Ibid., 153.

"self-communication" and "self-expenditure."[8] The argument of his work, *The Celebration of Flesh*, subtitled *Poetry in Christian Life*, is that only when the Christian lets go of his or her own particular and Christian concerns can poetry come alive and be of genuine significance. One must divest oneself of a "Christian agenda" in order to be receptive to what poetry has to give on its own terms.[9] In McGill's words, "The poems of Eliot or Frost or Stevens have value for the Christian provided he submits to their spell; provided he does not try to be self-consciously religious."[10]

McGill is working with a literary-critical analogue to Incarnation, an "incarnational hermeneutics" which kenotically opens itself to otherness:

> Poetry provides a constant help against . . . [a] closed off, self-secure kind of Christianity. . . . To be sure, things in their immediate impact may distract a person with their dazzle and specious vitality. . . . But the antidote . . . is not to run away from immediate experience, but to bite into it more deeply, until its limitations and deficiencies burn on the tongue. After all, Christ did not overcome death by believing in a doctrine of resurrection, but by entering into death and concretely discovering its limits.[11]

McGill has the power to make ideas, concepts, differing perspectives vivid—to "in-flesh" them. He begins an essay on "Reason in a Violent World" with words from a motion picture advertisement: "Power-mad killers . . . notorious, untamed women clashing in a sun-scorched sin spot"[12] and so enlivens an entire outlook as backdrop before which his reflections maneuver. McGill likes to take on an issue "far back." He carefully prepares the ground,

8. See, e.g., 26, 29 below; *Suffering: A Test of Theological Method* (Philadelphia: Geneva, 1968), esp. 51, 68–73. The latter work has been republished with an appreciative and perceptive "Foreword" by Paul Ramsey and William F. May (Philadelphia: Westminster, 1982); see esp. their remarks, 11–13; 2nd ed. Eugene, OR: Wipf and Stock, 2006. (All references to this work in the present essay are to the 1982 edition, though the page numbers in the 2006 edition remain the same.) See also Gilbert C. Meilaender's reference to McGill in relation to "self-expenditure" in Meilaender, *Friendship: A Study in Theological Ethics* (Notre Dame: University of Notre Dame Press, 1981), 50–51.

9. In conversation, the contemporary Irish poet Micheal O'Siadhail remarked, "Am I a Christian poet? I am a poet." McGill would approve.

10. Arthur C. McGill, *The Celebration of Flesh: Poetry in Christian Life* (New York: Association Press, 1964), 188; 2nd ed. Eugene, OR: Wipf and Stock, 2009.

11. *Celebration of Flesh*, 188–189. Note in this connection Michael Peterson's reference to McGill's work in *Evil and the Christian God* (Grand Rapids: Baker, 1982) 17.

12. Arthur C. McGill, "Reason in a Violent World," in *The Distrust of Reason* (Middletown, CT: Wesleyan University Press, 1959) 34. For another example of McGill's ability to carve out a distinctive perspective, see McGill, "Ambiguous Position," 107.

sets the stage, and does so in a way which makes the matter to be dealt with even more intractable than his readers or hearers might have imagined.

Then comes the "switch" or reversal or inversion empowered by the very confrontation McGill has arranged. For instance, after referring to a view associating God with "order" and rehearsing the powerfulness of the "demonic" as "that peculiar energy of destruction" on which newspapers thrive, McGill asks:

> Do Americans, then, worship two different and opposite kinds of divinity–on Sunday morning a good God, who stands behind this good world, and during the rest of the week demonic powers, which run through the earth and destroy?[13]

By this time we are, perhaps, ready to venture an affirmative response. Just here McGill turns the tables: "I find little evidence that this is the case, that Americans are being pulled religiously in two opposite directions. And the reason is obvious. For most people the old background God does not really exist any more."[14] It's worse than we thought. McGill leaves only the demonic as the object of our worship. Just when we supposed that he was about to come to the defense of this "world-governing, background God"[15] he dismisses such a God, leaving us with the demonic, leaving us room to affirm our own doubts and perplexities, leaving us with a harsher formulation than we might have ventured, leaving us attentive to what he is going to do next and to where he is going to lead us. Because by now we are following him.

---

13. Arthur C. McGill, "The Power of God and the Problem of Suffering" (unpublished lecture series at Princeton University, 1963), I-13 (this means Lecture I, p. 13; McGill begins the page numbers anew with each of the six lectures). I refer to these six lectures with some hesitation. McGill writes in a brief "Preface": "In view of the informal character of all this material, I would like it understood that it is to be kept strictly within the local Princeton scene, and treated only for what it is, not finished theology but some rough and ready sketches of a theological topic." Much that is contained in these lectures McGill later reworked and published as *Suffering: A Test of Theological Method* (see n. 8 above). Moreover, I find something of his compelling power more effectively captured in the "rough and ready" character of these lectures than in some of the more "finished" work. McGill would surely want to call into question any reference to "finished theology" (though he himself refers to "finished theology" in contrast to "rough and ready sketches"); see "The Unending Nature of Our Quest" in *Suffering*, 128–30, where he declares, "All theology is provisional"—including his own.

14. Ibid.

15. Ibid., I-14.

Another instance of reversal: McGill argues that our society is in search of an "Elsie the cow" kind of God supplying every need, while the Christian God comes alive in the arena of death.[16] In an address on "The Crisis of Faith," he mocks the idea that the crisis of Christian faith is a problem of "packaging" and declares, "[Jesus] is not irrelevant to us; we in our social and personal values are irrelevant to him. The person who finds it hard to believe in Jesus is exactly the person who is beginning to know Jesus."[17] Then comes the switch. Far from seeking some remedy for our crisis of faith, McGill expresses the hope that it might grow worse, having done his best to help it to do so with a celebration of receiving, giving, and gratitude in the New Testament as distinguished from our concern for possessions and giving out of our surplus. He challenges us to enter into a situation of fundamental neediness in which we can receive and give and hence be ready to receive again and again and to live in constant gratitude thereby.[18] This model of Christian life as receiving and giving in gratitude is decisive for McGill's approach to divine power, death, and resurrection. As we will see, much of McGill's work centers on these considerations.

In an essay called "The Death of God and All That," the "All That" gives some indication of what McGill finally thinks of "Death of God" theology and suggests the playfulness present in his work.[19] McGill loves to say, "Emphasis is very often given to . . ." and "we will examine . . . elements . . . that indicate quite a different orientation."[20] McGill has fun with the footnotes to T. S. Eliot's *Waste Land*, proclaiming, "In the discussion that follows, I will not pursue . . . [the] customary allusionist method."[21] After quoting lines from Wallace Stevens—"The water puddles puddles are / And ice is still in Februar. / It still is ice in Februar . . ."—McGill asks, "Who cares?"[22] In the context of his own struggles for health, he is able to observe, "I'm

16. See Arthur C. McGill, "The Death of God and All That" in C. W. Christian and Glenn R. Wittig, eds., *Radical Theology: Phase Two* (Philadelphia: Lippincott, 1967) 57. Some of us remember Elsie the Borden cow, famously employed by Borden to advertise dairy products.

17. Arthur C. McGill, "The Crisis of Faith" (Pittsburgh: Thesis Theological Cassettes, January, 1974), vol. 4, no. 12.

18. Ibid.

19. See McGill, "The Death of God and All That."

20. McGill, *Dogmatic Theology*, 196.

21. McGill, *Celebration of Flesh*, 55. See also 97 and other examples of how McGill switches tracks and turns tables in "Reason," 39, and ch. III, 22–23.

22. McGill, *Celebration of Flesh*, 134.

now convinced after my operation that it's only the healthy that can survive the hospital."[23]

To invest in McGill's work is to discover increasingly that he is what Kierkegaard calls an "essential author" as contrasted with a "premise-author." A premise-author is "outwardly directed," while an essential author is "inwardly directed." An essential author "has his own perspective . . . he strives forward indeed, but within the totality, not after it. . . . The essential author is essentially a teacher."[24] Wholeness and unity characterize McGill's thought at a deep level, the wholeness of Incarnation-warranted self-expenditure, risk, openness, and freedom. Here is the source of McGill's power.

What is true of "power" holds for other touchstone terms in McGill's work: they are both transitive and reflexive; they both characterize his thought and characterize *him*—terms like "celebration," "enjoyment," "demonic," "dazzle," "radiance," "relish," "pilgrimage," "gratitude," "glory." Above all, glory. McGill became the arena (another of his favorite words) where these qualities came powerfully into play. McGill became the vehicle, the instrument, of his subject, as rich, as vast, as variegated—and as essentially needy—as the theology he rendered in playful exuberance and contagious fascination.[25] I propose we call it "McGillian glee."

On the "Place" of Death: Against Thanatolatry

One of McGill's strengths, well suited to our foraging present, is the nonidolatrous seriousness with which he confronts evil. In McGill's work, as outside of it, the demonic lives. McGill's theology of confrontation tries to take on evil and death[26] "full strength." At least part of the evil of death is its evil-engendering potential. Death invites the evil of what William

---

23. Arthur C. McGill, "Human Suffering and the Passion of Christ" in Flavian Dougherty, CP, ed., *The Meaning of Human Suffering* (New York: Human Sciences, 1982), 192.

24. Søren Kierkegaard, *On Authority and Revelation*, Walter Lowrie, trans. and ed. (New York: Harper & Row, 1966), 6–9.

25. I had forgotten this description of McGill's theology from the early 1980s when I proposed calling a series of McGill volumes, some twenty-five years later, *Theological Fascinations*.

26. A basic question, "Is death evil?" is not begged by McGill but bewildered with dialectical complexity—yes and no—by way of different concepts of death. See below, 13.

Stringfellow calls, in a phrase appropriate to McGill's concerns, the "idolatry of death."[27]

Death is worshiped when it is perceived as *extermination*. McGill takes extermination to be "termination" plus the "abolition of all possibilities."[28] Death as extermination elicits strategies of resistance. One such modern strategy is medicine, and McGill often observes certain religious intimations in the "consecration" of medicine.[29] More probing is his suggestion that investment in history, the rise of modern historiography, is to be understood as a strategy of resistance to death. If medicine seeks to ward off death (literally), history strives to negate death's negation, to undo death in recovering the past.[30] In either case, death is calling the shots: thanatolatry lives.

Thanatolatry may live otherwise. McGill perceptively sees how paradox haunts the Heideggerian call to build authentic life on the foundation of death.[31] There is the *negative thanatolatry* of resisting death at all cost and so bowing before death's domination, before death as extermination; there is also the *positive thanatolatry* of ascribing to death the source of all true life. McGill strives to warn against both.

In a volume on *Medicine and Religion*, McGill speaks in an informal discussion of his heart attack:

> I have always been absolutely convinced that my death was one of the most crucial elements in my destiny. Death is something that's mine. I never think of death as something that befalls me because of cancer or a heart attack. My death is the climactic event of my own personal biography.[32]

27. See, e.g., William Stringfellow, *Count It All Joy: Reflections on Faith, Doubt, and Temptation Seen Through the Letter of James* (Grand Rapids: Eerdman, 1967), 48–50. Wipf and Stock Publishers has performed a great service in putting the works of William Stringfellow back into print ("Bill Stringfellow: read him again–for the first time"). See Stringfellow, *Count It All Joy* (Eugene, OR: Wipf and Stock Publishers, 1999), 48–50. William Stringfellow (1928–1985) was an astute, trenchant theological critic of American society.

28. See ch. III, 49.

29. See ch. III, 52. See also McGill, "Reason," 41–42: "And the hospital—the place where the battle is joined and where the monstrosities of medicine meet the monstrosities of disease—is a holy place of awe and stillness, where the only people who can walk with safety are the white robed initiates, the doctors and nurses."

30. See ch. III, 51–52.

31. See ch. III, 56–57.

32. Arthur C. McGill, "The Religious Aspects of Medicine" in Donald W. Shriver, Jr.,

He says that he considered it a "temptation to depersonalize death, to externalize it."[33] These remarks make clear where McGill stands in relation to two "placings" of death which he elaborates in an essay on "The Religious Aspects of Medicine." One placing sees death as "decisive powerfulness" which overwhelms a person "from outside." Hence, death is circumstantial.[34] The other sees death as coming "essentially from my being."[35] McGill thinks that medical practice in this country proceeds according to the former view. But, he contends,

> when death is seen as a property of every person's being, it is not primarily an event in the circumstantial sense. The death which occurs at a particular time and place is not the aspect of death with which I primarily wrestle. The more essential aspect of death is a dimension of myself.
>
> With this sense of human mortality, death ceases to be an alien powerfulness from which we try to protect ourselves and ceases to be that which elicits our religious intentions. As a dimension of ourselves, our dying, like the other aspects of ourselves, only pertains to our way of being related to some kind of powerfulness.[36]

Is this "some kind of powerfulness" the power of death within us or the power of God to which we are to be related in dying as in "the other aspects of ourselves"? It is, I think, the latter; for McGill says that in "religions like Judaism and Christianity . . . authentic life depends exclusively on and is constituted exclusively by a proper relation to God."[37]

We might want to ask of the understanding of death as "a dimension of ourselves," what kind of death is this? How did death get "inside"? How is death related to God? Is one fighting God to fight death? Is death God's doing? Some of these issues will be touched upon below; but, for the most part, McGill develops the two views without asking the surrounding questions. Imaging the "place" of death as inside the self seems motivated by the concern to warn against thanatolatry. If death is located outside the self—as grim reaper, destroyer, exterminator—death may be separated from God's doing. Such "separated" death can, however, upstage God and

---

ed., *Medicine and Religion* (Pittsburgh: University of Pittsburgh Press, 1980) 78.

33. Ibid., 81. But see McGill, "Ambiguous Position," 116.

34. McGill, "Religious Aspects," 92.

35. Ibid.

36. Ibid., 92–93.

37. Ibid., 89.

9

appear almighty. McGill pronounces, "Neither cancer nor accident nor war nor death, but only the Lord is God; only He holds the lives of men in His hands. That is why the first and second commandments hold good."[38] Such anti-thanatolatry is secured in McGill's reading of Jesus as one for whom death is *not the decisive* problem of life.[39]

Finally, if death is located outside the self, passivity can result. Passivity may be the response to death "inside" the self as well; but at least when death is inside, one can address it, do something with it, *act*. McGill stresses Jesus' *activity* in dying,[40] for to see Jesus as but a "passive victim" would be to set God's kind of life and the death which Jesus dies in competition. But *are* they not in competition? Not at all, challenges McGill. We have arrived at one of the most fascinating turns in his theology.

Resurrection as Receptivity: Against Demonolatry

The active Jesus on the cross shows us "how to nurture love in the presence of death."[41] This is the heart of McGill's teaching—and the heart of Christian life as well as Christian death. How do we nurture love in the presence of death? Resist building walls around the self, McGill replies.[42] Remain open to receiving and giving. Loving and opening, in fact, are the same heart and are directly related to McGill's theme of power. Power, the power of the Christian God, is opening and self-giving, and must be distinguished from dominative, demonic power. God's life and the death Jesus dies *cannot* compete with one another because, in one sense, they manifest and are different *kinds* of power and, in another sense, they are moments in one divine power and life.

McGill sees not death but life as coming to a person from outside the self. In *The Celebration of Flesh*, he celebrates poetry as "the language of flesh" but makes clear that this has nothing to do with elevation of appetites over ego or ego over appetites: "The shadow of death embraces them both alike, so that men do not find life simply by freeing one of these from all restraint. *Life lies outside of them both.*"[43]

38. McGill, ""Reason," 47.
39. See ch. III, 62–63.
40. See ch. III, 68–69.
41. McGill, "Reason," 50.
42. See McGill, "Human Suffering," 180–82.
43. McGill, *Celebration of Flesh*, 19. Italics added.

A formal relationship obtains significantly between McGill's articulation of the gift of divine life continuously received by the creature on the one hand and the world that "gives itself to man in radiant openness"[44] on the other. Speaking of the "openness" and "non-veiledness" in persons, McGill attests:

> He does not have to close himself within his own existence, in order to preserve his identity. He can open himself to the identity of other things, by freely letting their existence, just as it is, fill his consciousness.[45]

Much that is indicative of McGill's thought is signaled here. McGill emphasizes that "openness on man's part is not a natural faculty or a matter of passivity, but an interior *act* of profound self-assessment."[46] Openness includes and *is* activity: "What suggests itself here is that we think of knowledge less after the analogy of vision than after the analogy of the dance, less as a static confrontation than as a harmony of reciprocal action."[47] Think what it would be like were we to respond to another's words, not with the metaphor so common that it is "broken"—"Oh, I see!"—but with "Oh, I dance!" This dance is one which would please McGill. I recall his concluding a lecture on agape in the late sixties by quoting approvingly a little verse of Abner Dean called "Grace Note":

> Remember the word–?
> The one from the manger–?
> It means only this . . .
> You can dance
> With a stranger.[48]

McGill warns against "the poverty of needing nothing"[49] in reference to "The Night Song" of Nietzsche's Zarathustra:

> I do not know the happiness of those who receive . . .
> This is my poverty, that my hand never rests from giving . . .
> Oh, craving to crave! Oh, ravenous hunger in satiation! . . .

44. McGill, *Dogmatic Theology*, 37.

45. Ibid., 41.

46. Ibid., 44. Italics added.

47. Ibid., 47.

48. Abner Dean, *Wake Me When It's Over* (New York: Simon & Schuster, 1955), 59. Abner Dean (1910–1982) was an American cartoonist and writer.

49. McGill, *Dogmatic Theology*, 73.

> Oh, the loneliness of all givers! . . .
> Alas, thirst is within me that languishes after your thirst.[50]

McGill's trinitarian God does not have this problem. Not to be in need is to be self-enclosed, walled-up, but empty: this is the true life of neither God nor persons.

The life of the university, too, is the life of "giving and receiving,"[51] according to McGill; as it is giving and receiving which characterizes the life of God, the life of Jesus, the true life of the human creature.[52] Furthermore, McGill includes an analysis of death within the "soteriological" framework of the university, where all "objective reflection" involves "an experience of death"[53] which is "only the precondition of an experience of life."[54] Death and resurrection in the university! My point is not that this is theologically reductive but that it presents an unmistakable formal parallel to McGill's handling of Christian themes. Thus a person's existence is "relational,"[55] and "genuine interaction means the gain of identity for one thing and a corresponding loss of identity for another."[56]

Possibly such "secular" epistemological reflection has found shaping ways into McGill's theology. Possibly McGill's theology of death and resurrection has affected his rendering of reason's quest. Possibly, as "essential author," insight amicable to openness, otherness, neediness, and the movement of receiving and giving lies behind both.

A bold reading of Jesus' life and death is joined recurrently in McGill's writings; a concept of what might be called the "dynamic substantiality" of the self or even "trinitarian personhood" results. McGill speaks of the "ecstatic identity" of Jesus[57]—an identity standing and coming from outside himself—and locates "the center of Jesus' reality"[58] in a way which moves both beyond thanatolatry and beyond what I shall call "demonolatry." He

---

50. Friedrich Nietzsche, *Thus Spoke Zarathustra* in *The Portable Nietzsche*, trans. Walter Kaufmann (New York: The Viking Press, 1954), 218–19.

51. McGill, *Dogmatic Theology*, 74.

52. I observe McGill's order here, "giving and receiving"; though, humanly, Christianly, receiving precedes and is the precondition of giving.

53. McGill, *Dogmatic Theology*, 109.

54. Ibid., 111.

55. Ibid.

56. Ibid., 112.

57. See ch. III, 62–68.

58. See ch. III, 63.

says of Jesus: "There was no moment and no regard when, to himself or to others, he was simply the reality which he possessed, simply his own self. Always and in all ways he was receiving himself from God."[59] McGill develops this in trinitarian terms and is aware of concentrating on the giving and receiving of Father and Son to the neglect of the Spirit.[60] Further, Jesus' dying is "the *gift* of his life to us."[61] Jesus' death is "an event of glory."[62]

What is going on here? Has not thanatolatry won the day—and the life? We must make an implied distinction between death as extermination, the stinging death of sin claiming worship (see 1 Cor 15:55–56), dominative, demonic death, and death as, in McGill's words, "communicating expenditure."[63] This latter death is true death and is an ongoing moment in the true life of receiving and giving; from this death Jesus did not retreat even as he did not draw back from the demonic death of extermination.[64]

After reminding us that we are to live without walls, McGill adds: "But in a world where the rule of God is not yet complete and where a demonic powerfulness still moves at large, this abandonment of walls means the acceptance of suffering."[65] We must ask about this "rule of God." Meanwhile, the statement indicates that McGill is not beholding suffering—and death as extermination—as desirable in themselves or as essential ingredients in

---

59. Arthur C. McGill, "Suffered Under Pontius Pilate–Theological Brief," in Robert A. Evans and Thomas D. Parker, eds., *Christian Theology: A Case Study Approach* (New York: Harper & Row, 1976) 149; see also ch. III, 65.

60. See esp. McGill, *Suffering*, 64–82; see also McGill's comment regarding the omission of the Holy Spirit from the discussion, 128. But see McGill, "Power of God," III-1: "God is a mystery of self-communication within himself, a continual and everlasting act of self-conferral where a) the Father is constantly generating the Son and is constantly conferring his whole reality and glory upon the Son and b) where the Son is constantly offering all that he has received back to the Father, and c) where the Father acts toward the Son and the Son acts toward the Father by means of the same self-communicating activity which is called the Holy Spirit."

61. See ch. III, 69.

62. See ch. III, 69. See also McGill, "Power of God," V-7.

63. See ch. III, 69. See also McGill, "Power of God," III-13.

64. See McGill, "Human Suffering," esp. 181–182. Does Jesus suffer two kinds of death upon the cross, a death demonic and a death divine, a death of sin and a death of creatureliness, a death which leads nowhere and a death which leads to life? One death is sounded in "My God, my God, why hast thou forsaken me?" (Mark 15:34), the other in "Father, into thy hands I commit my spirit!" (Luke 23:46).

65. Ibid., 179.

true life. Suffering is present because "This is not yet my Father's world"[66] and because the rage of evil is on the loose.

But if this is so, how can McGill say, "There, not in the resurrection, but there on the cross, is the decisive and overwhelming and unimpeachable triumph of God's power over evil and sin"?[67] Two questions emerge stubbornly. First, how is the cross victory? Second, *if the cross is victory*, what is "left over" for resurrection to do? How can we construe resurrection without treating it as but a delayed expression of demonic, satanic, dominative power? How does God win and "rule" without losing God's character as the God of self-communication in the process?

Christian theology is constantly and in many guises threatened by the temptation of the "delayed zap": you can get away with murder now, but ultimately God will get you! Now God's powerfulness is manifest as suffering servant and self-giving love; but then God will show you who is who and what is what and what real power is. But this "real power," McGill argues, is precisely what the world has been calling power all along: the power to dominate, the power to obliterate. The resurrection is construed as God's victory in the sense that God's power is *greater* than the power of death. Yet "greater" suggests the same kind of power but more of it. God is the winner and still champion of the world—on the world's terms. In his *Love in the Western World*, Denis de Rougement refers ironically to "the fidelity of all those Tristans who are really Don Juans in slow time."[68] McGill forces us to ask, "Is the Christian God dominative in the end time?" (Is God an apparent Tristan who, eschatologically and in truth, is a Don Juan?) Do we avoid thanatolatry only to capitulate to "demonolatry"? By "demonolatry" I mean the hope and expectation that God will exercise dominative, demonic power to obliterate death and the wider rage of evil. Is not demonolatry, I wonder, alive and well in Christian faith and expectation?

McGill writes, "In the passion . . . Jesus was not controlled by fear and did not attribute to destructive forces a power comparable to God's."[69] Here is our clue to the way in which crucifixion can be seen as victory quite apart

66. McGill, "Human Suffering," 176.

67. McGill, "Power of God," V-7.

68. Denis de Rougement, *Love in the Western World*, trans. Montgomery Belgion (Garden City: Doubleday, 1957), 321.

69. McGill, "Human Suffering," 181. Note the ambiguity of "comparable" in this passage. I am suggesting that McGill wants to assert a qualitative distinction between demonic and divine power: "comparable" does not mean "as great as" (quantitative) but "of the same kind" (qualitative). McGill must mean "comparable" in kind.

from resurrection. Crucifixion is the victory of the true form of life, of an open, receiving and giving, vulnerable, "no-walls" life, even in the presence of ruthless destruction. The victory is that destructive power has not caused true personhood to retreat into wall-up defensiveness. The destructive evil of crucifixion tempts one to draw back into attempted self-possession. Jesus nurtures love even in the presence of death.

"I am the resurrection and the life," says Jesus in the fourth Gospel (John 11:25), where cross and victory are one and where McGill is at home.[70] True life is receiving all life from God. McGill explains:

> Through Jesus our identity lives not within ourselves but in the constant receiving of ourselves from God. This means that we *are* not our present lives; we who are this receiving from God only "have" our present lives. We are not the same as our lives.[71]

The other side of receiving all is giving all. Losing one's life for Jesus' sake is not the condition for finding one's life: it *is* one's life. The rage of evil destroys this rhythm, this dialectic, in death. Resurrection stands as jolting incursion in an evil-infested world. In the kingdom, however, resurrection is not dramatic reversal of death but a recurring moment in the life of receiving and giving, where giving is not vulnerability to demonic death but vulnerability to divine life.[72]

We have arrived, finally, at the question of resurrection, where the McGillian reversal is—that there is no reversal. McGill asserts:

> The cross represents the victory of God, and the failure—though not the abolition—of satanic pretense. What the resurrection adds to the cross is this abolition. For on his return from death, Jesus is portrayed as existing wholly outside the realm where death

70. The fourth Gospel claims a special place in McGill's thought. Therein, McGill interprets, death is not extermination but "the process of generating and communicating life" (see ch. III, 69). McGill cites John 12:13—"In truth, in very truth I tell you that a grain of wheat remains a solitary grain unless it falls to the ground and dies; but if it dies, it bears a rich harvest." (Dostoevsky chooses these words as the epigraph for *The Brothers Karamazov*.)

71. See ch. III, 70. If God holds our lives, we are free to live with a certain abandon. Only as we let go can—will, does—God get a grip on us. See McGill, "Theological Brief," 148–53; see also "Power of God," II-4.

72. When demonic power collapses, resurrection is not "intervention" but what happens continuously in the rhythm of the divine life. See McGill, "Power of God," VI-10.

operates. Dominative power, with all of its pretenses, is here done away with completely.[73]

McGill has rightly rejected the familiar view that "After losing the first round to the devil, so to speak, God came back after three days to win the fight."[74] Such a relationship between crucifixion and resurrection is disastrous for McGill, because it suggests that God and the devil are not only in the same ring, fighting the same fight, but fighting it in the same way: by means of dominative power. Paradoxically, for God to win with demonic power is for the demonic to win, for God to demand—and to justify—demonolatry.

McGill sees the issue clearly. He speaks of "the defeat of Satan, or the destruction of death"[75] and cites 1 Corinthians 15:26: "The last enemy to be destroyed is death." He focuses upon the Greek verb translated "destroyed" (καταργεῖται) and says:

> Now the word "destruction" here makes it sound as if, in the age to come God would become dominative and violent, and would defeat Satan by satanic means. Actually, the word which Paul uses here, *katargesis*, does not mean to destroy something in a context of force. On the contrary, it means to make idle, to make barren, to render inoperative, to bring to nothing. In the age to come, then, death is not destroyed, as if it really had genuine substantive power and could only be removed by violent attack. No, death is simply evacuated, impoverished, so utterly emptied that it vanishes. Perhaps the best word is nullified.[76]

Demonic death is what happens when the life of receiving and giving is invaded by the false "life" of holding and keeping, of domination. Apart from demonic death, the dynamic would—and will—continue as it truly is: the zest and joy and freshness, the heartbeat of the divine life itself. Death seems to halt this heartbeat, while in fact it but exposes the condition of its continuance.

73. McGill, *Suffering*, 97.
74. Ibid.
75. McGill, "Power of God," VI-9.
76. McGill, *Suffering*, 97; see also "Power of God," III-3.

-❧

I hope Arthur McGill might have recognized something of himself and of his concerns in these words. Were he to read them, I should be both delighted and uneasy—and, above all, anticipatory. I would be still more attentive, so that I should miss nothing. And I wonder if "lo! In a trice everything would be changed." If "in a twinkling everything would be inverted." Again.

The Work of Arthur Chute McGill

(Arranged Chronologically)

"The Twilight World of Popular Songs," *Religious Education*, XLIX, 6 (November-December, 1954), 382–88.

"Reason in a Violent World" in *The Distrust of Reason: Alumni-Faculty Seminar: June, 1959* (Middletown, Connecticut: The Wesleyan University Press Incorporated, 1959), 34–50.

The Place of Dogmatic Theology in the University (Ph.D. dissertation, Yale University, 1961).

"The Power of God and the Problem of Suffering" (Series of six lectures delivered at Princeton University, 1963).

The Celebration of Flesh: Poetry in Christian Life (New York: Association Press, 1964), 2nd edition Eugene, OR: Wipf and Stock, 2009.

"The End of Intimacy" (East Lansing, Michigan: Christian Faith and Higher Education Institute, 1965).

"The Education of the Specialists," *The Christian Scholar*, XLIX, 1 (Spring, 1966) 24–32.

The Many-Faced Argument, ed. with John Hick (New York: Macmillan: 1967), 2nd edition Eugene, OR: Wipf and Stock, 2009.

"The Death of God and All That" in C. W. Christian and Glenn R. Wittig, eds., *Radical Theology: Phase Two* (Philadelphia: Lippincott, 1967) 45–58. Also published in Walter D. Wagoner, C. Shelby Rooks, and Robert P. Montgomery, eds., *Essays in Ministry* (Princeton: The Fund for Theological Education, n.d.) 10–23.

"Technology and Love—A Human Problem" in *Man in Nature and the Nature of Man*, Fifth Combined Plan Conference, Arden House, Harriman, New York, 5–8 November, 1967.

Suffering: A Test of Theological Method (Philadelphia: Geneva, 1968; Philadelphia: Westminster, 1982)

"Critique II," *Theology Today*, 25 (1968) 317–19.

"Is Private Charity Coming to an End?" in *Vanguard: A Bulletin for Church Officers*, 6 (1969) 3–6, 16.

"The Ambiguous Position of Christian Theology" in Paul Ramsey and John F. Wilson, eds., *The Study of Religion in Colleges and Universities* (Princeton: Princeton University Press, 1970), 105–38.

"The Crisis of Faith" (Pittsburgh: Thesis Theological Cassettes, 1974).

"Structures of Inhumanity" in ed. Alan M. Olsen, *Disguises of the Demonic: Contemporary Perspectives on the Power of Evil* (New York: Association Press, 1975), 116–33.

"Suffered Under Pontius Pilate—Theological Brief" in eds. Robert A. Evans and Thomas D. Parker, *Christian Theology: A Case Study Approach* (New York: Harper & Row, 1976), 148–53.

"The Religious Aspects of Medicine" in ed. Donald W. Shriver, Jr., *Medicine and Religion: Strategies of Care* (Pittsburgh: University of Pittsburgh Press, 1980), 77–93

"Human Suffering and the Passion of Christ" in ed. Flavian Dougherty, C.P., *The Meaning of Human Suffering* (New York: Human Sciences, 1982), 159–93.

Death and Life: An American Theology, eds. Charles A. Wilson and Per M. Anderson (Philadelphia: Fortress Press, 1987), 2nd edition Eugene, OR: Wipf and Stock, 2003).

Sermons of Arthur C. McGill, ed. David Cain (Eugene, OR: Wipf and Stock, 2007), Theological Fascinations, Volume One.

Dying Unto Life: Arthur C. McGill on New God, New Death, New Life, ed. David Cain (Eugene, OR: Wipf and Stock, 2012), Theological Fascinations, Volume Two.

Editorial Note

I mainly repeat here the "Editorial Note" from Volume One—with changes and additions. I am most grateful to Lucy McGill for entrusting to me so long ago, on the recommendation of William F. May and Paul Ramsey, the papers of Arthur McGill; to William F. May for granting me "the McGill files," for his patience and encouragement; to Paul Ramsey for his caring and kindness; to Chuck Balestri and Egbert Giles Leigh, Jr., friends since Princeton undergraduate days (some fifty years), to Chuck for many rewarding McGill-catalytic or McGill-catalyzed conversations at Princeton, 1960–1963, when we were both under McGill's spell, to Egbert, biologist at the Smithsonian Tropical Research Institute, Barro Colorado Island,

Panama, for his enduring interest and encouragement; and to Wipf and Stock Publishers, Christian Amondson, Heather Carraher, Rodney Clapp, Charlie Collier, Ted Lewis, Jim Tedrick, and associates, for their continuing investment in Arthur McGill. For finding (or trying to find) information requested "out of the blue," I thank Lorraine Fuhrmann, Department of Religion Manager, Princeton University, Princeton, New Jersey; Linda Hall, Archives Assistant, Williams College, Williamstown, Massachusetts; Kyungmi M. Kim, Office of the Registrar, Princeton University; Angela Kindig and Peter Lysy, University of Notre Dame Archives, Hesburgh Library, Notre Dame, Indiana; Peggy Roske, College of Saint Benedict / Saint John's University Archivist, Alcuin Library, St. John's University, Collegeville, Minnesota; Karen Shea, Library Manager, The Hastings Center, Garrison, New York; and Leah Whitehouse, Registrar's Office, Harvard Divinity School, Cambridge, Massachusetts.

Here "at home" at University of Mary Washington, thanks to Cindy Toomey, Office Manager, Department of Classics, Philosophy, and Religion (CPR), a valiant assistant in sundry ways; Liane Houghtalin, Professor of Classics, CPR; Gary Richards, Assistant Professor of English, Department of English, Linguistics, and Communication; and Peter Catlin, Evening Reference Librarian, Simpson Library. Carla J. Bailey, Interlibrary Loan Supervisor, Simpson Library, has been a helpful colleague and friend for decades. Once again she has come through patiently, efficiently, expertly, in supplying rare and odd texts. Thanks again, Carla. My immediate colleagues and friends of some twenty-five years, Jim Goehring, Professor of Religion, and Mehdi Aminrazavi, Professor of Philosophy and Religion, CPR, have, as always, been insightful, helpful, and supportive.

When Arthur McGill penciled, often rapidly—one can see the acceleration of the writing in his hand—a vast paper trail of theological fascinations, he did not know that persons someday would struggle to decipher his difficult and often minuscule hand. He was about his own present, pressing, and remarkable intellectual adventures. Still, the little sheets paper-clipped to larger sheets clipped to note cards in sometimes thick and puzzling disarray are thwarting. And the abbreviations . . .

The concern here is to respect the text. "Man" and "he" and "him" are untouched. Commas and semicolons posed a temptation: add some, subtract others. With rare exceptions, punctuation-wise, spelling-wise, capitalization-wise and otherwise (and apart from possible misreadings of the manuscripts), the texts have been permitted to stand. When manuscript baffles or temptations triumph, there are brackets [ ]—different kinds: 1) [word?] means this is an uncertain but best-guess reading; 2) [?] means there is a word, but I haven't a clue; and 3) [??] means more than one indecipherable word. When the manuscripts become outline or word-notes, I have risked making coherent connections, again within brackets. Originally, every added "a," "the," "we," "our" and infrequently added punctuation mark were dutifully placed in brackets. Brackets, brackets everywhere. I decided to do away with the brackets in the case of articles, etc., but retain them in the case of other additions. (I have "cheated" on some punctuation marks.) There are too many brackets, and every set of brackets is (for now[77]) a defeat. Often the manuscripts slip into "inverse paragraphs": instead of indentation of the first line, lines under the first line are indented. This accounts in part for many of the short–and one-sentence–paragraphs; though at times I have created paragraphs. Then there are the dreaded outlines and infinitesimal marginal notes.

McGill uses different translations of scripture, the Revised Standard Version (RSV), and, quite often, The New English Bible (NEB). Sometimes there seems to be no exact fit, and no translation is designated. The version may well be MM = McGill's Memory. When a text is indicated but not quoted by McGill, the RSV is used—unless McGill's words operate off of another translation.

I have retained such references as "this morning," "in these lectures," "in this paper," "this evening," "Thank you," "On Wednesday," "right now here with you," "Let me read," etc., to serve as reminders of the spoken and circumstantial and varied character of the texts.

Different papers and lectures have different structures, different section divisions—numbers, letters, asterisks—different titles, etc. I have respected them and have not made them all alike. The "chapters" are thus variously articulated. I have sought to make references uniform. References in parentheses in the text are McGill's. References in brackets in the text are mine. When McGill employs brackets in the text, this is indicated. In the notes, McGill is clean (no parentheses, no brackets). My notes are in brackets unless the note is obviously mine.

I have noted the numbers of the file-folder homes of the materials from which this volume has been assembled in the hope that one day

---

77. Often I have stared at a word with magnifying glass for extended times over days—and over years. Then, suddenly, the word is clear and unmistakable. A little victory. Lucy McGill has been responsible for many such victories.

McGill's manuscripts will find a place in some institutional library where they will be available to interested persons.

In mid-July of 1973 at St. Peter's Episcopal Church in Port Royal, Virginia, C. FitzSimons Allison preached one of the finest sermons I have heard. We have been friends at a distance ever since. I am grateful for his perceptive and appreciative "Foreword" and proud to be associated with him in this way.

I

Inverted Values

Death as Occasion for Nourishment Anew[1]

We are what we receive. Need means that what we receive becomes us. Many have put themselves into me. How to give when aware of need? Don't we back off from others? [Yes,] if having, possessing is the answer to need. But in the Kingdom of the Parenting God, possession is not finally necessary. Possessions already have their reward.

Communication of life to others, to the human race—that is the glory of Jesus' dying. But that power, that capacity to extend and generate and communicate life does not originate with Jesus. He, too, only receives it from God the Parent. This is also the supreme disclosure of God's character and glory. If the Christian community worships God, it worships a God who is essentially and properly Parent, who essentially and properly is as the act of generating life. And therefore the Christian community's worship is called forth by the supreme event of God's communication of life—the communication that takes place at Jesus' death on the cross. There is darkness cast out of the world. There does the character of God's power and being shine out. There does God the Parent manifest his glory.

If we have become new creatures through Jesus Christ, if we exist in a new way, if, at the center of that new way is the realization that we are constantly from the Parent (as Jesus said of himself), [?] we are children of

---

1. The notes and text I have edited here come from file folder #145 labeled "From John: mode of interaction / Good lecture." I have chosen the title, lifting it from the text. Parts of this lecture overlap with parts of the concluding ch. 5 ("In Christ the Love of the Neighbor Involves—Death") in Arthur C. McGill, *Death and Life: An American Theology*, eds. Charles A. Wilson and Per M. Anderson (Philadelphia: Fortress Press, 1987); 2nd ed. Eugene, OR: Wipf and Stock Publishers, 2003. Yet much of this lecture is distinctive. I have been unable to find a date.

God, and the realization that we are born of God as a constant process of being given ourselves by God—if this is a relationship to God as the center of our new nature, this becomes actual for us through Jesus' extension to us of this new life, this new relationship to God which was the center of his being.

We share and experience ourselves in this way because, by dying, Jesus extended to us, communicated to us and constituted in us this way of being, of which he is the origin and fullness. People exist with the nature of Jesus, because—and only because—Jesus died. From this perspective, therefore, Jesus' death is the supreme actualization of the character of God as Parent, as life-giver; for it is the event by which we became receivers of this new way of being, this new and grace-given identity. For us to share Jesus' nature, the day of his death is not just Friday; it is certainly not black Friday or dreadful Friday. The day of Jesus' death is Good Friday, through which Jesus' Parent God becomes our Parent, our continuing Parent, and through which we become new creatures. Jesus' death is our birth as God's children and therefore is our becoming vessels of God's glorious communication of life. The Christian church could never have taken any other symbol than the cross.

[Jesus is speaking:]

> "But woe to you that are rich, for you have received your consolation.
>> "Woe to you that are full now, for you shall hunger.
>> "Woe to you that laugh now, for you shall mourn and weep.
>> "Woe to you, when all men speak well of you, for so their fathers did to the false prophets." (Luke 6:24–26, RSV)

The rich fool amassed wealth and died on the night he was to begin enjoying his wealth (see Luke 12:13–24). [Consider the] slave to two masters, God and money. Or Lazarus versus the rich man (see Luke 16:13–31, Matt 11:12f, 5:31f, Mark 10:11f). Where your treasure, there your heart (see Luke 12:32–34, Matt 6:19–21). They have their reward (see Matt 6:2, 5, 16).

This morning I wish to examine two aspects of this supreme event of the communication of life, this event through which we receive our new natures and God vindicates the divine glory in us and to us.

The first aspect of this: what does it mean that, in order for Jesus to communicate life to us and nourish in us the kind of nature which he had, the kind of relation which he had with the Parenting God, Jesus had to die?

The answer, I think, is immediately obvious but staggering in its import. The answer is that Jesus existed, the being and reality and knowledge and vitality which Jesus found as himself when constituted continually by God's grace—he existed to extend all this beyond himself to others. He was constituted with his own life for no other reason than to communicate that life out of himself and into others. In other words, (in my view) Jesus' death shows that the communication of Jesus' reality to others, for their nourishment and new being, necessarily entailed his losing it.

Remember, of course, he does not thereby lose the taproot of his identity. He is from the loving, generating action of the Parenting God; he is not from the reality which is in him and as him. His identity is rooted in the Parenting God and constantly comes from God. But he does lose all the reality that does lie in his possession: not the root and center of his reality, which are outside his possession in God the Parent and not in himself, but the concrete substance and present possessed content of his reality. All of that he dissipates from himself, he lets go from himself, to be taken into the being of others.

Jesus is not given life for himself. He is given life to give it away. And giving it away to others entails his losing it. You can see that, for this viewpoint, the process of eating is such a useful and illuminating way of construing Jesus' life. Because at the level of animal life, no animal can exist without eating some other living reality. An animal must take in plants or other animals in order to be. In that perspective every animal exists to be eaten. Its being eaten is not one of the unfortunate indecencies by which vicious nature violates our enlightened modern sensibilities. Its being eaten is its crucial purpose. No plant or animal exists just to be itself. It also exists to nourish other animals, to die and be eaten so that the life in it passes beyond it to others animals. That passing beyond, that nourishing and communication requires it to die.

This is the analogy which the early church quickly brought into play to characterize Jesus' death or the communication of life. He died so that we might derive a nourishment of new life, new possibilities, from him. And his dying is no unfortunate accident. It is no product of human sin which we, of course, would never allow to happen. On the contrary, this is the supreme aim and goal of Jesus' existence. This is supremely what he received his existence for, to give it away, confident that he would receive it again because his Parenting God would not cease to Parent. His communicative dying when he hands over his life to us—that is what he refers to when he says: "It is accomplished" (John 19:30, NEB). That is the goal and fulfillment of his existence. His life moved out of him and into others.

Now I am going to make a proposal. My proposal is this: that when we look upon Jesus' death as the communication of life and see that deathly communication as the goal of his actual active concrete living, then we have a model for understanding the character of all dynamic human action. Let me explain.

If we take the old, basic, normal way of human existence, the way of existence by self-achievement, self-domination, and self-possession, action in this context has a clear and crucial role: action is a person's defense and extension and solidifying of his or her own possessed reality. Action is behavior, and behavior serves the basic life-project of actualizing the reality which constitutes my being. All dynamic outward projects, all energetic activities that involve the self going out into the world, are ways of extending the self, reaching out in taking possession for the self of some object or person or situation to which the action is directed. It involves modifying the world for the benefit of the self. There often is an exchange: to be able to extend myself, to be able to direct my energy into a situation and take possession of some bit of it for my reality, I will have to let others take possession of other bits of a situation. If I speak in a conversation to actualize myself at that place and at that moment, I will have to let others also speak. But this pattern of exchange is a necessary development when two agents interact so that both move to actualize themselves. By activity I move in terms of my problematic reality. I can extend it, impose it, secure things from the world for it.

It is precisely this use of activity which Jesus' dying puts in devastating question. For what if it were the case that Jesus' death shows us the true and final meaning of human activity? I mean this: suppose that in every activity which I do, in every effort I make to move with purpose, energy, self-investment out beyond myself into the world—suppose that by that activity pieces of my reality were thereby passing out of me into the objects and situations and persons on which I directed my activity. Supposing all action were controlled, not by the law of self-realization, but by the law of self-expenditure and of self-communication. Suppose right now here with you my active work of speaking to you represented the movement out of me, beyond me of some of my reality, some of my own reality which is at my disposal. Suppose that for every agent its actions are all dissipations of itself.

Then death appears in a new light. Then death is not the robbing of a person's life by some disease or accident or alien force. Rather death is the proper and essential outcome of action, the accumulated undoing and dispersement of a person's being by the actions over much time.

Jesus' death, I think, sets the activity of those who share Jesus' way of being in this perspective. Every action is a losing, a letting go, a passing away from oneself of some bit of one's own reality into the existence of others and of the world. In Jesus Christ, this character of action is not resisted, by trying to use our action to assert ourselves, extend ourselves, to impose our will and being upon situations. In Jesus Christ, this self-expending character of action is joyfully affirmed. I receive myself constantly from God's Parenting love. But so far as some aspects of myself are at my disposal, these I receive to give away. Those who would live as Jesus did—who would act and purpose themselves as Jesus did—mean to love, i.e., they mean to expend themselves for others unto death. Their being is meant to pass away from them to others, and they make that meaning the conscious direction of their existence.

Too often the love which is proclaimed in the churches suppresses this element of loss and need and death in activity. As a Christian, I often speak of love as helping others, but I ignore what this does to the person who loves. I ignore the fact that love is self-expenditure, a real expending and losing and deterioration of the self. I speak of love as if the person loving had no problems, no needs, no limits. In other words, I speak of love as if the affluent dream were true. This kind of proclamation is heard everywhere. We hear it said: since you have no unanswered needs, why don't you go out and help those other people who are in need? But we never hear people go on and add: if you do this, you too will be driven into need. And by not stating this conclusion, people give the childish impression that Christian love is some kind of cornucopia, where we can reach to everybody's needs and problems and still have everything we need for ourselves. Believe me, there are grown-up persons who speak this kind of nonsense.[2] And when people try to live out this illusory love, they become terrified when the self-expending begins to take its toll. Terror of relationship is [?] we eat each other.

But note this very carefully: like Jesus, we too can only live to give our received selves away freely because we know our being is not thereby ended, but still and always lies in the Parenting of our God. Otherwise we

2. See McGill, *Death and Life*, 88.

unleash by our self-expenditure a nightmare of oppression and obligation. For we can know of no oppression so terrible as that of having imposed on us by others their painful self-sacrifice for our sake. Sacrifice and expenditure for others are among the nastiest and the most devastating sources of power and tyranny. If to serve you I really undo myself in some final and fundamental sense, then by that act I have a weapon over you before which you may find it very difficult to defend yourself. Jesus died. Jesus expended the life at his disposal. This involved great relative pain. But this was essentially by him a positive life-full act. This was his glorifying, not his undoing. And therefore nowhere in Christian experience do we find expression of a sense that Jesus is pressuring, mastering, and manipulating us by the dreadful agony he suffered for us. On the contrary, his so-called agony was not only his glory but our glorious new birth as well. Destruction simply does not figure in this perspective.

Now let me turn to the second aspect of Jesus' death. Not only must Jesus give his life: we must receive it. His dying not only entails his giving, it also entails our receiving. This means that we do not simply consent to Jesus' death in a passive way. We act dynamically to take the life from him and into ourselves.

It is the need for this active cooperation on our part which is expressed in those passages in John which sound cannibalistic. You must eat my flesh and drink my blood [see John 6:48–58]. It is not enough for Jesus to direct his life to the fatal communication of it. We who live from him must actively take from him that life which he gives. According to the deliberately offensive expression in John's Gospel, we must eat his body and drink his blood [see John 6:53]. It is certainly not the case that our Eucharist is a memorial of the last supper. That view is a perversion which wants to keep us away from Jesus' death. The Eucharist is the reactualization of Jesus' death but with one crucial addition: with the addition of our eating and drinking, our active taking in of the life which Jesus is losing and giving away. It is we, by our act of eating and drinking, who make Jesus' death into a meal. Without that his death would be barren. We must eat and drink. We must open ourselves and take in his life, his vitality, knowing that this is only possible by means of his death, knowing that only if he really lays down his life and expends it from himself can it really leave him and truly enter us.

But how can we do this unless we sense that we need this life, that we are hungry and that we are true, not only to his loving gift, but also to our own selves by taking his life from him and into ourselves?

In my judgment, this is a much more critical problem than the first issue. To live beyond ourselves and to expend ourselves for others is not unthinkable. It sounds like a super achievement, has a certain attraction. But to be needy, to act out of need, to act out of such need that we take life from Jesus, we eat his body and drink his blood—this is much more difficult. To know that my aliveness is nourished by the radical self-expenditure of others for me and into me, this is almost beyond us.

Death represents the absolute evil. But right here we may, I think, understand this difference in a clearer light. For it is not death itself which is the basic issue. The basic [issue], rather, concerns an essential aspect of our human nature: the aspect of neediness.

When we identify life and well-being with holding and possessing ourselves and whatever we require, neediness then becomes the primary evil. To find, within the boundary by which we mark what is our own reality, that we do not have what we need—this is most terrifying. We work to remove our neediness, for this neediness forces us to be open and seek help and in that way to depend on what lies outside of us. Our neediness declares: you do not possess and hold yourselves. To remove our neediness we simply expand the circle that is ourselves and that has our name on it to include whatever we require. Since we cannot do this privately and individually, we form communities, so that the community owns everything we need. We have security, we ourselves possess and have disposal over everything our existence requires, not privately, but through the community. In this perspective, to need and not to have is the abomination. Death simply proves beyond a shadow of a doubt that neediness without possessions is utterly destructive.

In the Kingdom of Jesus, however, there is a new kind of identity which he brings, where we are called to receive, to take in. This kind of living is in tune with the foundation of reality. The new identify in Jesus therefore might be described as a becoming one with our neediness—with a neediness which constitutes our fundamental relation to God. In the Kingdom of Jesus, when I speak of a life of love, a life when we are able to let go of all that we have received so that it may go and nourish others, I am describing human activity as a response to the neediness of others. And when I stress the importance of our participating in Christ's death by our eating him, I am locating a fundamental need and hunger in us. When, in the light of Jesus' cross, I observe how self-expending love may entail our death, may involve us in losing all possessed identity, losing all that is within the circle of ourselves, then I am describing the conclusion of human activity as a movement toward extreme neediness. In short, in the Kingdom of Jesus, we always begin with neediness, we always live outward toward neediness and we always end in neediness.

From the viewpoint of this kind of life, evil appears in two forms. Basically it appears as our trying to suppress within ourselves any hint of our neediness. But it also appears in our abusing rather than nourishing others who are needy. Both kinds of behavior have the same source. In the first form of evil, where we try to live by our capacity to possess, we act so that our own neediness will not affect us. In the second form of evil, when we ignore or dominate or exploit or ravage those who are in need, we act so that the neediness of others does not affect us or control us. In either case, with the rich as with the oppressors, life is essentially a refusal to be affected by neediness. And this perspective crowns itself with the worship of a God who is cut off from all neediness.

Why such opposite judgments about neediness? Why in the one perspective is it found intolerable, and in the other perspective fully accepted? The difference is the love of God—no, the difference is the God who is essentially Parent and Offspring together, who is engendering and communicating and receiving life, who is love. If this Parenting God is the creator and lord of reality, then we have no fear of need. God's perfect love has cast out all our fear [see 1 John 4:18]. But if reality is alien, then poverty and neediness represent conditions when we are utterly defenseless against barbarities, mutilation, and loss.

Too often in our churches we hear the gospel of love without the gospel of need. Too often we hear the lie that to love is to help others without this having any effect upon ourselves. And too often we hear, not that Jesus Christ enables us to be needy but that he enables us to be loving and by loving to remove all neediness. Christian churches today are full of the gospel of human loving; the gospel of Jesus' ability to make us unselfish, empowering us to nourish and sustain and liberate our needy neighbor; the gospel of the power of the Christian spirit to remove need from the human condition.

But that is not the gospel of Jesus Christ. Nowhere does Jesus promise the removal of need. On the contrary, he promises to each of his followers the intensification of need. He calls them to take up his cross [see Matt 16:24, Mark 8:34, Luke 9:23]. He warns them that it is only so far as they are willing to be poor and sick and needy that he can help them, for, after all, those who are healthy have no need of a physician [see Matt 9:12, Mark 2:17, Luke 5:31]. Blessed are the poor [see Matt 5:3, Luke 6:20].[3]

What is the real meaning of Christian love when obviously Jesus expects that love is to be exercised by those who are needy, and who know and accept their own neediness? What is the character of this love which can be known only by those who are constantly and joyfully grateful to God—that is, only by the poor?

The answer can be put simply: the love to which Jesus calls us is never the removal of need but the companion of need. Love serves need without removing need. Love does not want to give so that the other has no more use for love; love wants to give today, but only for today, so as to be able tomorrow to meet tomorrow's need.

But even that way of putting is not strong enough. Those who love in the name of Jesus Christ do not simply serve needs continually. No, those who love in the name of Jesus Christ serve the needs of others willingly, even to the point of being exposed in their own neediness. They begin in constant need, in which state God nourishes them. They are directed by Jesus to expend all that nourishment upon others, and so to end in need again. And there they must await another's help. And it is their need—and not their love—that relates them to God, and relates them to their neighbors. They do not cope with their own needs. They do not anguish over how their own needs may be met by the twists and turns of their circumstances, by the whims of their society, or by the strategies of their own egos. At the center of their life—the very innermost center—they are grateful to God, because there they let themselves be needy for God. And there they do not fear neediness. That is what frees them to serve the needy, to companion the needy, to become and be one of the needy. Even the final neediness— even the condition of death is, in the light and life of Jesus Christ, only another occasion for God to nourish us anew. Therefore, if persons love, in the way that Jesus Christ loved, that is, as the children of God, then they love as their way of dancing from neediness to neediness.[4] They begin with a beseeching and they end with a beseeching; they end their activity of

3. The following is scratched out: "But what of Jesus' call to serve our neighbor? If his gospel relates us to the goodness of God in such a way that we learn to accept our neediness, will we not be unprepared to obey his command that we serve the poor, nourish the hungry, give up both our shirt and our coat, and even lay down our lives for our friends [see Matt 5:40, 19:21, Mark 10:21, Luke 3:11, 6:29, 18:22, John 15:13, 21:15–17]?

"We now come to the heart of the matter."

4. See McGill, *Death and Life*, 92–93.

service sick or tired or defeated or demoralized or dead. And they do not fear this or avoid this. For this is simply that condition where they receive, that condition where they truly are to share in the life of God as receiving.

This means, then, that in Christian compassion, in Christian service to the weak and the needy there can be no trace of pity.[5] Pity is a corrupt attitude. It expresses contempt for those who are in need, and it expresses smug superiority in those who feel it. The Christian does not nourish the poor because he feels sorry for them. How can he feel sorry for weakness and need when these are his own essential condition and when these are the necessary conditions for the joy of receiving? In the United States, need degrades a person. Failure condemns a person—but not in the Kingdom of God. To be in need is to be in a condition of honor. The needy must not be pitied but honored, because they bear that condition which unites us with God and dignifies us as God's children and which in that dignity unites us to one another. Woe to the person who degrades the needy with pity. The needy are to be honored in and because of their neediness, just as Jesus is to be honored upon the cross, when his destitution attains its final form. Because we honor those in need, we nourish them as we can, letting ourselves be instruments of God's blessing and by our service and self-expenditure joining with them in need.

To see life in this way is obviously to turn normal values upside down, to champion that state of need which is usually found to be terrifying, and to condemn that state of wealth and having which is usually found to be fulfilling. In other words, to see life in this way is to realize how inverted are the values of the world, and how life is caught in a web of destruction because it seeks values of wealth and strength and love that are no values at all.[6]

---

5. See ibid., 93.

6. Scratched out: "Such is the tragic sense of ordinary existence which is opened up to us by Jesus Christ." Then: "In my next two lectures, I will be speaking of the two forms of having: the having of possession and the having of virtue or goodness." I have yet to succeed in putting the announced lectures together with the present text.

II

The Positive Meaning of Need

Revolutionary Gratitude[1]

"To be able to put our names on nothing..."

Christic Exchange and the Positive Meaning of Need

Let me consider the shape of human existence in the light—and in the life—of Jesus Christ. For how else can we define a Christian except as someone who sees in Jesus Christ the proper shape and form of human existence? Of course there are many phony Christians, who use Jesus Christ to prop up their own vanity, to reinforce their own sense of life, to assuage their own fears. For such people Jesus Christ is just a wax nose that they twist in any way they want. They have their understanding of life, and they expect Jesus Christ to fit into that. But for his followers, Jesus Christ is a revolution, a transformation. He himself—and not their own experience—becomes the measure of what life truly is. He himself becomes their center, and they seek to fit into him, instead of having him fit into their values. He is their beginning and their end. He is their way and their truth and their life [see John 14:6]. He is their judge, who challenges and discredits so much that they think is valuable and good. And he is also their comforter who holds and

---

1. This chapter comes from file folder #96 marked "Paper on Death at Williams." There are manuscript pages among other materials (three groupings of small sheets of notes—12, 7, and 10 pages, unnumbered). One manuscript set (an outline and 29 pages with small sheets stapled in) is headed "I. The Positive Meaning of Need." Hence, the title. I have added the subtitle, based on the paper. Neither Williams College nor I have been successful in finding a date. The epigraph following the title I have added also, taking it from the text.

sustains them when they have been stripped of all these tawdry supports on which they had been taught to build their lives, when they had lost confidence in their parents, had lost trust in their husbands and wives, had lost hope in their children, had seen the essential triviality of their work, had had exposed the emptiness of their pretenses by which they had bolstered their egos through the days. Jesus Christ is their rock, and Jesus Christ is their goal.

This fundamental attitude, where a person looks to Jesus Christ for the proper shape and final meaning of his or her life—this attitude is, I think, what Paul is describing when he wrote to the Christians of the city of Colossae. Let me read the passage from the third chapter:

> . . . now . . . you have discarded the old nature with its deeds and have put on the new nature, which is being constantly renewed in the image of its Creator . . . There is no question here of Greek and Jew, circumcised and uncircumcised, barbarian, Scythian, freeman, slave. But Christ is all, and is in all.
>
> Then put on the garments that suit God's chosen people . . . [Put on] compassion, kindness . . . patience. . . . And be filled with gratitude. . . . Whatever you are doing, whether you speak or act, do everything in the name of the Lord Jesus, giving thanks to God the Father through him. [Col 3:9–12, 15, 17, NEB]

Here Paul speaks of putting off the old human nature and putting on the new human nature which comes to us through Jesus Christ. People who live by the old nature, Paul observes, try to be real by acquiring an attribute which gives them an identity, any identity which relates them to some people and which also sets them over against other people. They try to be Greek or try to be Jewish: they try to be this or that, rich or poor, tall or short—they try to find something that will be theirs, that will be their own, some quality or property that they can possess and that can organize their daily lives, telling them what people they are like, with what people they can have a fellow-feeling, and also telling them what people they are unlike, to what people they are alien.

Paul calls for the Christians at Colossae to abandon this style and manner of life, and instead to put on the nature of Jesus Christ, to live the life in Jesus, full of compassion and kindness and patience and gratitude. That, Paul explains, is what it means for us to do everything in the name of the Lord Jesus. To do something in the name of Jesus is not to follow our own ideas of life and just add the name of Jesus to them—our American ideas of life, or our affluent middle class ideas of life, or our feminist ideas of life, or our super educated ideas of life. Not at all. To do something in the name of Jesus means to do something with the sense of life and the shape of life as Jesus lived it because we have put on Jesus, because with regard to our existence, the existence we do ourselves and share with others, and with regard to the organization of that existence which we are and share with others, we have let Jesus be its origin and its form, or in Paul's words, we have come to acknowledge that "Christ is all, and is in all" [Col 3:11, NEB].

This fundamental way of existing, where a person looks to Jesus for the fundamental shape and final meaning of his or her life—this attitude is identified by Paul in this passage with our attitude of *gratitude*. "Whatever you are doing, whether you speak or act, do everything in the name of the Lord Jesus, giving thanks . . ." [Col 3:17, NEB]. Thanksgiving pervades every corner, every dimension of this way of existing. This is why, I think, we are right in saying that this way of existing is *identified* with gratitude. Gratitude is not one of the things that happen[s] after one becomes a Christian, is not one of the virtues and attitudes which result[s] from putting on Jesus Christ. Gratitude is identical with this condition. To put on Jesus Christ is as such to be grateful. That is to say, the center of a person's gratitude is not what happens to him *after* he has put on this Christic way of existing, because now he realizes that all the things of his life have been given to him. The center of a person's gratitude is the putting on of this new way, this new existence.

In other words, there are strictly speaking two levels of gratitude. There is the gratitude we feel as we move out and with the world—and here gratitude is called forth when anything comes to us. In another place, Paul writes, "What have you that you have not received?" [1 Cor 4:7]. Anything—talents, life, ideas, friends! "But if you have received all things, why do you boast as if they were your own?" [1 Cor 4:7]. But prior to this level of gratitude that belongs to our dealing with the world, there is another level: we are grateful that we have put on Jesus Christ, that we [are] beloved of God and have Jesus' own kind of existence. We are grateful that we now live in such a way that we can be grateful in all our interaction with the world. In short, we are grateful for ourselves; for this new self we are that cannot only recognize how much it receives in all its dealings with the world, but in the face of that knowledge can feel gratitude.

This is one of the major themes throughout the New Testament. Jesus Christ does not only enable us to see our lives with our neighbor and with our world in a new light, as full of gifts. He enables us to see ourselves in a new light, as a gift from God—and as this new self to be worthy of God, pleasing to God, and called to behave and to act and to hope and to serve as a child of God, as one whom God has made worthy of his goodness and his love for the world.

But surely this cannot be the case. Surely I simply am. This body proves I am. My reality is now in my control. No! For no creature of God has his reality transferred into his own control. All creatures are continually being sustained by God. For us humans, this means that we are constantly receiving—ourselves. That gift to us of ourselves is the gift that precedes all others and underlies all others. We do not make ourselves. Our ambitions, our education, our parents, our country, our religion, our worlds—these do not make us. These are not our creators. God makes us, but in a peculiar way: he gives us ourselves. Not any self: a self worthy and capable of God's glory, of being children [a child] of God. That is what we receive, that is what we are. Think of it: we receive ourselves each day, each moment from God. And not [the] [?], bedraggled, twisted self our parents try to give us, our society tries to give us, or we try to give ourselves. We continually receive a self that belongs to and enjoys and does justice to the Kingdom and glory of God. All Christian ethics presupposes this fact and appeals to our awareness of this fact. If it appeals to anything else, it is not Christian ethics. Paul's image is important, however. The new self and new sense of ourselves is a matter of "putting on" Jesus Christ [Col 3:10, 12, see Gal 3:27]. It is ours as we let Jesus Christ be our Lord, our shape. If I look into myself isolated, I don't see that self: where is this exalted self? Jesus Christ is the actualization, the image of the kind of self God gives each of us. And God in fact bestows this self. If we look into ourselves, we see not what God gives us, but what society or our friends or our parents or what we ourselves try to give us. Jesus Christ is not only true God but also true person, the kind of true person God is now bestowing on each of us through Jesus Christ.

In a good deal of Christian life today there is very little attention given to this gift to us through Jesus Christ of ourselves. There is instead a one-sided secularistic preoccupation with what I am calling the secondary level of gratitude, that is, with gratitude in our dealings with the world. Jesus Christ, we hear constantly, gives us attitudes for coping with our neighbor and with the world, for helping our neighbors and improving the world, for our projective and active and creative life. Today in our churches we hear almost nothing of how through Jesus Christ we are given ourselves.

Two sad consequences result from this one-sidedness, this neglect. The first is that people are taught by the churches to look in the wrong place for the experience and the joy of love. The primary love, the foundation encounter with love occurs at our very center, in our inmost being, in this event of receiving—ourselves. My love for others and the [love] of others for me is secondary. Before I seek love from another, before I even dream of going for help to another, I am already loved in a most decisive way: through Jesus Christ I am given myself as something worthy of God. And before I love another and go to him to offer help and honor, he has already been loved in a most decisive [way]. Before I ever appear on the scene, he is the one to whom through Jesus Christ God has given a self worthy of fellowship with God. Of course, that relation to God through Jesus Christ which involves the gift of the self is not magical. The church, the neighbor are involved as God's instruments. But we begin our Christian life with that effected: with the gift of ourselves.

It is so sad, therefore, to hear the churches teaching people that they must go out into the world in order to find love. For love, they are told, go out to find a man or a woman to cherish; for love, go out to find a community to immerse in. Sadly enough, in their search for love out in the world, they miss their most profound experience of love: the love of God in giving them themselves.

To find love, begin by going into yourself and by going toward your neighbor or toward the world. For if you do not first rejoice in God's gift to you of yourself, of yourself as capable and worthy of his Kingdom and presence, you will never find adequate love from another creature. In spite of education and family training and processes of socialization, no human being, no human community and no cosmos can give you yourself. God and God only is your creator.

Something else happens when the Christian community speaks only of Jesus and of gratitude in our dealings with the world and neglects God's gift to us through Jesus Christ of ourselves. What happens is that God himself disappears.

Paul's words that I read from his letter to the Colossians are remarkably clear: it is to God and God only that we direct our gratitude. Whatever you are doing, do everything in the name of Jesus Christ, giving thanks to God through him. Jesus Christ does not come to commend our parents to us, or our society to us, or humanity to us, or the cosmic process, or even to commend himself. He comes praising God only (there is none good but

God alone [see Mark 10:18, Luke 18:19]), commending us to God alone (preserve them in thy care, O Father [see John 17:11, 15]), and thanking only God. And the radical priority which God has in our gratitude is grounded on the fact that in Jesus Christ he does not give us this or that, a law or a degree or a community. He gives ourselves, so that as ourselves we may be able to receive other things and to give to other[s] things in his name.

But if we forget this, if we disregard the fact that it is ourselves which we and others receive from God and for which we thank God, then God can only figure as one who gives us, already existing, this or that worldly blessing. Then gratitude to God can only be related to what I call the Thanksgiving Day syndrome. I look around in my existence for all the worldly items I have received, I carry through the secondary level of gratitude, and I attribute them to God.

And of course it's phony. When we receive food or shelter or medicine, do we actually feel gratitude to God, or to the farmers and the mortgage company and the physician and drug company? The problem is dramatically presented by a little boy down the street,[2] whose father works in a General Motors assembly plant. The boy is excited when his father promises a new Chevrolet: "From Daddy's own company!" In church on Sunday during a time of thanksgiving, the boy says, "Thank you, General Motors, for our new car." His mother whispers, "We don't thank General Motors. We thank God." At home in the afternoon, admiring the new car in the driveway, the boy remarks how wonderful it is of God to give us this car and asks, "Does God make all cars?" The father: "Not God exactly. Metal, design, etc. . . ."

Is God better [than?] General Motors? A dreadful confusion. God does not give us Chevrolet cars to win our gratitude, and he does not give us a self adequate for, worthy of Chevrolet cars. Here middle-class affluence has simply substituted itself for the glory of God in Jesus Christ, and imagined that its own existence represents the greatest thing God ever did. That is contemptible. A God who gives me Chevrolets and dubious parents and ambiguous friends and asks me to share these with others—is that what motivates Christian life? Let's hope not. What we receive from God, what marks God off in our gratitude from General Motors or Mommy and Daddy or the United States of America is that he gives ourselves, and ourselves are shaped to a new kind of existence, the existence actualized in

2. Here McGill resorts to notes, which I have tried to turn into text.

Jesus Christ and derived from Jesus Christ. And enjoying Chevrolets, when many of our brothers and sisters are too destitute to walk, is not part of it whatsoever.

No Third Item[3]

Up to this point I have been trying to describe the character and focus and basis of a particular kind of gratitude. It is gratitude aroused by and maintained in connection with Jesus Christ. But it is gratitude not to Jesus Christ, but through Jesus Christ to God. God is the exclusive agent whose giving arouses this particular gratitude. And it is gratitude to God for his action of giving us ourselves, the particular self and the particular way of life we have which we receive through Jesus Christ.

All this, however, is only preliminary. For it leaves out one crucial element, and this in fact is the element on which I will concentrate in these lectures. It leaves out the resistance which this kind of gratitude provokes in people. It leaves out how unattractive and disagreeable this particular gratitude appears from the normal and commonsense point of view. It therefore leaves out the change—or better, the revolution—which this gratitude entails for human life. Too often Christian gratitude is construed as if it were a perfectly normal human activity. Does not God like to give? Do not people like to receive? Is not gratitude, i.e., that perfectly natural and inevitable attitude which any decent person would adopt in the face of God's giving?

This, I believe, is an illusion, and it is an illusion that must be abolished. God's giving is not like ordinary giving, and receiving from God is not at all like ordinary receiving. In fact, it is just the opposite. Until this illusion is abolished, everything that I have said up to this point about Christian gratitude—and Christian love—will not be recognized.

Let me begin with this question: What attitude is necessary in order for a person to feel gratitude freely and willingly, and not reluctantly or begrudgingly? What is necessary is a willingness to receive, to take in to one's own existence something that originates from elsewhere, something that belongs to another and is bestowed by that other. To feel gratitude, it is not enough for another to give willingly to us. It is also necessary for us to receive willingly from that other.

3. McGill has not titled this second section. I have allowed the text to suggest a heading.

But right there, right at this point, lies the difficulty. In order to receive willingly, it is necessary to be needy: if we do not recognize our need, we cannot be grateful for the gift, however willingly and freely it may be given to us. For instance, if you feel that you ought to create your own self, as the great project of your career, then you will not be grateful to God if you [?] [try] to give you yourself. On the contrary, you will be indignant.

All gratitude involves this difficulty. You have to be needy. In normal life, however, we develop a beautiful way of minimizing that difficulty, that irritation and shame. True, in order to receive willingly, I must let myself be needy, must acknowledge myself to be needy. If I go to the doctor, to the teacher, to the church or to the store for the sake of receiving something, I have to recognize that I need it. But usually I can bring myself to recognize this, because by receiving, I cease to be needy. In fact, the only reason that I turn outside myself in my need is in order to receive something into myself, into my existence or into my possession that will take away my need. In other words, my need is temporary, and the process of another's giving and my receiving exists only for the sake of removing my need. "I receive" means that I now have what before I lacked. The need which drove me outside of myself to receive from another now finds its satisfaction in that which is *mine*. I needed food, so I went and had food delivered to me. I really *received* food. The food became mine to use. With that food I satisfied my hunger. I needed companionship, so I went, found a woman, and by a social process and personal persuasion and institutionalized custom had that person brought into my existence, made coincident with my existence. She became *my wife*.

This is the familiar process. Therefore, because receiving removes my neediness, because it confers upon my existence that which I require, I do all myself to acknowledge that I am needy—but only for a moment. Understand this clearly: I acknowledge myself to be needy before another and let myself receive from that other, only because I expect that this receiving will remove me from needing that other any more. The food for my hunger is now effectively mine. The wife for my hunger is now legally and psychologically mine. The need that I acknowledge in normal receiving is only temporary, and in fact is acknowledged only for the sake of being eliminated. If I went to another to receive food and then couldn't be sure that I had enough control over it to eat it whenever I wanted—if I went to another to receive companionship and then couldn't ever be sure she might walk away free from any claim by me—I wouldn't call that giving or receiving. And if I thought that that would happen, I certainly would not go through the unpleasantness of acknowledging my neediness.

So it is with normal receiving, and with the gratitude aroused in someone by normal giving. So it is with Thanksgiving Day, with the giving I may receive from General Motors, from Mommy and Daddy, from my country. In some sense, what I need is, by the act of giving, conferred upon my existence; and my needing no longer drives me beyond myself to another. Now that I have received, what I need I have within my own sphere.

Now we can understand normal gratitude. I feel thankful because what I require to meet my need has been given to me. In other words, in the process of giving and receiving, there is a third item—the *what* which I need, and which this process confers from another to me. My gratitude, therefore, is essentially focused on the conferral into my existence or on the possession by me of that third item, that what. My gratitude is my joy that I have what I need and am no longer being driven by my need beyond myself. By the process of giving and receiving, my "self" has been redefined, enlarged, expanded to include the "what" which I require.

It is precisely in this way that God does not give and we do not receive through Jesus Christ. Giving and receiving between God and humanity in Jesus Christ is not the transfer of some third item, some "what" which passes from the possession of God into the possession of humans. God gives us a new self by which we belong to him and reflect his will—his loving, his knowing, his serving. He never delivers this new self into our control and our disposal. This new self is never ours; it is his. It remains his and not ours; therefore, quite properly, it reflects his will and not our will. In Jesus Christ, God does not bestow himself upon us, so that he belongs to us and whenever we need him we have him. There is no having at all. And in Jesus Christ, God does not bestow ourselves upon us, so that we now belong to ourselves and whenever we want to be ourselves we already possess ourselves.

In relation to God, his giving and our being constituted in active receptivity involve no third item. We are constituted by his activity, by his giving, by his continual giving, by his continually giving his life to us and ourselves to us. We never have these delivered over to us.

In this connection, think of our nakedness and destitution in relation to God. We are nothing, absolutely nothing. All that we are is being received from God, and never established or owned for one instant by ourselves. Certainly this can be a source of unlimited gratitude, as Paul insists. And because gratitude is a form of joy, certainly we can give God not only our gratitude but also our praise, that his glory should be sufficient for our life and our joy. But this human destitution can also be a source of uncontrollable fear. To have nothing, to receive nothing into our possession, to be able to put our names on nothing: to be only receivers—isn't that threatening and dismaying? I do not want God to give me myself. I want to make myself, I want to be my own achievement. And I will be angry if God tries to give me myself in such a way that I never own myself. "Sorry, God," I will say, "but I am not going to receive myself from you. I am not going to be that weak and needy. No, sir! I am going to make myself, so that I can be on the cover of *Time* magazine." The point I wish to stress—and it is a point that will keep reappearing in my lectures here—is that Christian gratitude is not like secular, worldly gratitude at all.

All secular and worldly giving involves conferring something on us, in our possession, in our control, in our being. It thus makes us independent. Gratitude is our feeling of joy over the fact that we have ceased to be needy. But God never gives in such a way that, after he has given to us, we then own his gift for ourselves and can walk away with it as if it were our own. To be grateful for this divine kind of giving, to praise God for everything that is his and always remains his—this is the miracle of the Christian life, of which the world, including the nice charitable world of decent people, knows nothing at all.

As I read the New Testament, I am struck increasingly with how gratitude is the taproot of the Christian life. The gospel which Jesus Christ brings and which Jesus Christ is serves primarily to set people in the posture of gratitude, and from that posture of gratitude issue all the Christian virtues and all the Christian freedoms.

But if that is so, if Jesus Christ reveals a God who is merciful and nourishing and who calls us to share in his own life, and if Jesus Christ is the perfect form of our new humanity because in all things he is grateful to the Father, then the essential meaning of Christian redemption is that human beings may rejoice in—their neediness. For Christian gratitude can only exist where neediness is freely acknowledged and joyfully accepted. In normal gratitude, need is not accepted. Need is rejected: we acknowledge need by receiving from another only because we believe that his giving and our receiving will remove our need. But in Jesus Christ, need is met by God, not by the conferring of something into our possession. With Christ we continue to need and to have need met. That is why Jesus Christ may lead people into gratitude only if he enables them to accept their own neediness joyfully. Why does Jesus live a life of such gratitude? Because, as he said, all that I have and all that I am I receive from the Father [see John 3:35, 6:57, 16:15]. Because he was willing and delighted to be weak and needy in himself, and in his weakness and need to be nourished by the Father. So also in the light of Jesus Christ, the Christian also rejoices in his neediness, because that is the indispensable condition for his being grateful to God's bounty.

This constant need, this unremitting need for what is not ours and never becomes ours—this alters everything which I said in my description of gratitude. First, it alters the character of God's giving. For this means that when God gives, nothing is delivered over into our control. There is no third item, no "what" that is transferred from God to us so that we now possess what we need. We never possess what we need, but are continuously receiving it, are continually existing open to his graciousness. "God's giving" is therefore a very dangerous phrase. God gives only in the sense that he relates people to himself. He does not give in the sense that he confers something over to them so that thereafter they have no need of him.

In the second place, this alters the significance of need. In the normal perspective, "need" is terrifying; need is the most terrifying human condition. To have nothing, to be driven to dependence and beyond dependence to nothingness—this is the final terror. But in the perspective of Jesus Christ, need is the supreme good. Need is the condition which relates us to God. In connection with that glory and magnitude that is represented as God, there is no conferral, no transfer of ownership from God to humanity. There is simply humanity's need by which it clings to God.

Therefore, in the third place, this Christian "gratitude" is very different from normal gratitude. This gratitude has no concern for anything being delivered into human control. It is gratitude to God, to him for his nourishing, for his being our God, for his constituting us as selves that may be conformed to Jesus Christ and pleasing to him. Therefore it is gratitude that includes our neediness, it is gratitude that we may be dependent and not independent, that his giving works so as to hold us to him, and does not work so as to confer some third item into our control which leaves us independent of him. It is gratitude that we may be continually grateful, continually in a neediness that can be satisfied only from beyond ourselves and never in ourselves. In short, it is gratitude that we are delivered from normal gratitude, from that gratitude which fears neediness above all other conditions, and free from a gratitude which therefore rejoices only in wealth, only in whatever third items can be delivered over into our possession, freed from a gratitude that rejoices only in being redeemed from neediness. Christian gratitude is necessarily directed not just upon what we receive—the blessings of God—but also upon our own unrelieved neediness that makes [us] always receptive of those blessings.

What is faith? It is the confidence that God is sufficient for our neediness, that there is no neediness to which we can be driven which cuts us off from God, which surpasses God's communication and power for us. Faith is the faith to be needy in ourselves, because constantly enriched by God.

What is the fear which God's perfect love casts out [see 1 John 4:18]? The fear from which Jesus delivers the human race? It is the fear of neediness, the fear of not having.

Obviously, this whole series of reflections points to that decisive condition where faith and fear are established: the condition of death. On the one hand, death from the normal point of view is the condition which proves that need is destructive. Death is neediness carried so far and so destructively that here the self or the society is simply exterminated. Because of death, we know that need is evil, that reality will not nourish us, that we will live only so long as something is delivered into our control. Death proves that need must be feared.

But on the other hand, from the perspective of Jesus Christ, even death, even that final neediness is only another occasion when God nourishes anew. Death simply shows the essential emptiness of the creature wherein he depends upon God for all his being. Death discloses the extent of having—its total vacuity. Death is therefore that neediness in which the creature always stands to his creator, in which the children of God always stand in relation to their Father. Death is the disclosure of yawning need, of total need which remains the creature's in and through all God dealings with him. You have nothing and can be at all only so far as you continually receive.

In our country, we do not look with favor upon need. We like to think of ourselves as a nation of bronzed people:[4] skin so bronze, clothes so clean, smile so self-assured, property so sufficient that any trace of need and dependence is removed. The bronzed people, the rich people, are a lie. Because having is not the proper relation to what we need. Openness, dependence—but not possession. The bronzed person is the person who

4. "Bronzed people" is a pervasive image in McGill's oeuvre. See, e.g., McGill, *Death and Life*, 84–90.

owns what he needs. He is grateful—of course, he is grateful. He is grateful, because he has received in a way which he finds reassuring. That is, he has received in a way which frees him from needing others. If he is religious, he probably feels this same kind of gratitude to God. He probably believes that God has been responsible for liberating him from need for others and even for God. But this having and this gratitude are the lie. It is an illusion. God delivers nothing of decisive significance into our hands, into our possession and control. For the selves we are that carry the life ways of Jesus Christ, we are constantly dependent on him. For the life we have with one another we are inexorably inter*dependent*—not inter-autonomous, not grateful for possessions that free us *from* one another, but inter-dependent, dependent on one another without pause.

That is why the first beatitude is so profound: Blessed are the poor [see Matt 5:3, Luke 6:20]. Only the poor, only those who are willing to be poor and in their poverty are willing to receive from God, only they can enjoy the blessings of God That is why St. Augustine could write: "It is more blessed to be one of the poor than to serve the poor."[5]

What Jesus Christ does, then, is to disclose the sufficiency of God—not of God's gifts—but of God's own activity for human need. Not God's gifts but God is that on whom we depend. Faith is ever resting our neediness upon God and not upon his gifts. Therefore, in order for Jesus to redeem human beings and human communities, he relates them to the all-sufficiency of God's goodness to human need, and thus Christ enables people at last to become one with their neediness, to accept and affirm their neediness, as their primary and inescapable posture before God. A broken and a contrite heart [see Ps 51:17] is the only possible and the only worthy offering to the Father in our Lord Jesus Christ.

---

5. See St. Augustine, *The Works of Saint Augustine: A Translation for the 21st Century: Sermons III (51–94) on the New Testament*, trans. Edmund Hill, O. P., ed. John E. Rotelle, O.S.A. (Brooklyn, NY: New City Press, 1991), 213: ". . . I have become a beggar for the beggars. What's in it for me? Let me be a beggar for the beggars . . ." (Sermon 66: "On the Words of the Gospel of Matthew 11:2–11: When John in Chains Heard of the Works of the Christ, Etc.") See *Sermons of Arthur C. McGill*, 62 and n. 6.

III

Identity and Death

The Human Condition in Jesus[1]

I. The Contemporary Interpretation of Death

A. *The Prevailing Conviction*

Resistance to death appears to be a basic and universal fact of human life. The beliefs, the goals and the customs of all societies are informed by that resistance. It therefore might be called a "natural" attitude. Though it is unitary in terms of the event that it opposes, this posture of resistance actually is based on a variety of experiences. Three stand out with special prominence.

First, death is experienced as loss. It removes us from family, from friends, from the only social setting we have known, from the objects and tools and shelters that have become co-extensive with our living. Every human person lives outward into the world. People constitute themselves therefore, not in terms of what they possess within themselves, but in terms of a vital mental and physical dynamic toward what is other. Death seems threatening because it deprives them of that whole realm of otherness toward which they have actualized themselves. In some societies this sense of

---

1. The title is McGill's. The subtitle is mine, coming from the paper. The paper is found as typed manuscript in file folder #114 labeled "Hastings Paper" and folder #206 labeled "Hastings Paper on Death." I have not discovered a handwritten manuscript. "Hastings" refers to The Hastings Center, Garrison, New York—"a nonpartisan research institution dedicated to bioethics and the public interest since 1969." Both folders contain copies of the paper, complete and partial, with minor handwritten revisions. Other copies of this manuscript appear in other files, often as pages or partial pages cut and pasted (taped) into other papers, other contexts. I have been unable to date the paper. A good guess is 1974.

loss has been expressed by the conviction that when people die they enter a pale shadowy world of sterile impotence, a tenuous world devoid of dynamic vitality. In this experience death does not mean solitude so much as the evisceration of all satisfying activity. Even if after death I find myself in some kind of world, it will be a world that lacks that hard, dynamic, concrete otherness by which all my being as vital dynamism has been constituted.

Secondly, death is also experienced as a mutilation of one's being. It involves some deep wounding of the self's integral life-system. This wounding may come from without as a fatal blow. It may come from within as progressive decrepitude, as the gradual withering of the body by age or disease. The medieval images of hell may be seen as a projection beyond death of this experience of death as catastrophic mutilation.

Third and finally, death is further experienced as some kind of failure of human responsibility, with guilt and self-accusation. This sense of guilt need not have a legal form, as if some violation of an explicit law or moral principle were recognized. It involves a much more primitive anxiety, a questioning that, since the life of some person has failed, perhaps this happened because in the case of this individual we humans did not direct our life-resources in a proper way. Some societies focus this sense of failure upon the person who dies: death is taken as a mark of that individual's own sinning. But in other societies the question of guilt is laid upon the community as a whole, or upon those who were expected to have sustained the now dead person. In our society the medical and helping professions immediately—and, where there seems to have been a more long-term failure of responsibility, the family—are made the chief bearers of guilt. In any case, death is broadly experienced as confronting people with a question of whether and how they may have failed their responsibilities for life.

The prospect of loss and emptiness, the fear of mutilation and the burden of guilt: these are elements that nourish the posture of resistance. Though at a particular time a society may articulate only one of these agonies and may try to reduce the whole problematic of death to such narrower terms, all three are constant and universal components in the human awareness of death.

All this, however, only represents the first level of the situation. That is to say, this posture of resistance, along with the experiences that feed it, collides with two other factors which require this posture to be included and reinterpreted in a larger context.

For instance, however destructive death may be taken to be and however dedicated a resistance it may provoke, the fact of its inevitability cannot be ignored. Awareness of that inevitability must interact with and modify the initial impulse to resist. If death cannot be avoided, when and in what way and to what extent can resistance be pursued without becoming pointless?

Or again, however destructive death may be in certain regards, in other regards the loss of life may be experienced as a blessing and a good, as an event of change full of hope and promise. It is not simply that certain people's living entails intense physical pain and imposes acute deprivation ("Why did I not die in my mother's womb?" [Job 3:11]). It is also the case that our present existence burdens or disappoints even at its best. It involves such a constant expenditure of energy, such a drain upon the self that "I have been half in love with easeful Death . . ."[2] And the actual fulfillment which it brings seems so meager by comparison with the longings of the human imagination that revulsion cannot be avoided. The high imaginings, in fact, are taken as the intimations of a more exalted life beyond death. Therefore, however much an affluent society like ours may insist that humans should be satisfied and happy with their present existence and should see all failure, distress, and misery as merely private or temporary accidents, a sense of the inadequacy of this existence and a reaching beyond it remain in the consciousness. This perspective is voiced in a dialogue from ancient Egypt:

> Death is in my sight today
> (Like) the recovery of a sick man,
> Like going out into the open after a *confinement*.
> Death is in my sight today
> Like the odor of myrrh,
> Like resting under an awning on a breezy day.
> Death is in my sight today
> Like the odor of lotus blossoms,
> Like sitting on the bank of drunkenness.
> Death is in my sight today
> Like the *passing away* of rain,
> Like the return of men to their houses from an expedition.[3]

2. John Keats, "Ode to a Nightingale," in W. H. Auden and Norman Holmes Pearson, eds., *The Viking Portable Poets: Romantic Poets: Blake to Poe* (New York: The Viking Press, 1950), 384.

3. James B. Pritchard, ed., *Ancient Near Eastern Texts Relating to the Old Testament* (Princeton: Princeton University Press, 1950), 407, "Egyptian Didactic Tales: 'A Dispute over Suicide,'" trans. John A. Wilson.

If, then, the posture of resistance is a universal fact in human experience, it is a fact which humans must subject to further interpretation. For they must balance their initial impulse to resist, first, against the fact that death is irresistible and, secondly, against the recognition that the life which death kills may itself be impoverishing and destructive. Giving some kind of decisive order to this confusing mixture of awareness is the function of the overarching interpretation of death which marks every society. Such an overarching interpretation does not appear primarily through activities of intellectual reflection. It appears in the basic images of death that pervade a culture and in the concrete ways in which those images allow the life-energies of a people to interact with death.

If we ask about the overarching interpretation of our own society, there is one image that dominates the culture: death is *extermination*. This image construes death as an event which totally abolishes a human being. The element of "totality" is decisive. For what is emphasized here is not only that death represents the end of whatever being and identity an individual actually possesses. It also eliminates all the possibilities of his being and identity. I take it that what the word "extermination" adds to the notion of "termination" is precisely this abolition of all possibilities.

This means that the image of extermination reaches far beyond the empirical order. It functions mythically. It delineates what is true, not just in this present world, but in the realm of unlimited possibility. It specifies that death ends both the present actuality and every conceivable possibility of individual human being.

In terms of the mixture of confusing awarenesses which I indicated above, this interpretation builds exclusively on the posture of resistance. That is to say, by construing death as pure and total negation, it calls people to a single-minded resistance and silences the voices in them which would have them either submit to death as a necessity or seek death as a release.

I shall consider an alternative to this myth in the next section of this paper, but here I want to emphasize its way of shaping people's life-energies. For what this myth imposes is a *three-fold ethic*.

1. The fact that death is imaged as extermination means that it stands in total opposition to all being and becoming, to all life and all value, to all the affirmative possibilities of human existence. In short, it stands against every authentically human impulse. This represents a clear ethical mandate. It directs people to seek their entire reality and fulfillment in terms of their present visible existence. It is the value which energizes secularity.

2. The fact that death is extermination means that people should never relate to death in an affirmative manner. As the total obliteration of a human being, it cannot in any way be approached by motives, thoughts, or purposes that affirm human life. Any basic complaints about the possibilities of our present life, any hints of a death wish or of a longing for blessedness in some eschatological domain are seen as betrayals of the most decisive ethical value, as dangerous seductions which may tempt people to consent to that which negates every good and every possibility of good. The contradiction between death and the truly human is radical and absolute.

Paul Ramsey voices this form of the ethical mandate in his protest against the idea of "death with dignity."[4] Death, he argues, should never be taken as a "part of life,"[5] as one of the moments in life along with birth and growth,[6] as something merely natural.[7] It is the end of a totally unique, unrepeatable and once-for-all life-span.[8] It is "oblivion" and "nothingness,"[9] the conquest of being by non-being. Since death deprives people of "everything making for worth in this their world,"[10] it has to be acknowledged as "the loss of all worth."[11] Therefore it should be experienced only as "an ultimate indignity,"[12] and a phrase like "good death"[13] should be discredited as a flagrant contradiction.

People in general have carried the negative mandate which Ramsey emphasizes even further. As the abolition of everything human, death should not only not be domesticated as something natural and not be prettified as something dignifying. It should also not even be thought or spoken.

4. Paul Ramsey, "The Indignity of 'Death with Dignity,' " *Hastings Center Studies*, vol. 2, no. 2. (May, 1974), 47–62. Paul Ramsey (1913–1988) was a distinguished Christian ethicist who taught Christian ethics at Princeton University from 1944 until 1982. He and McGill were colleagues during McGill's years at Princeton, 1959–1968.

5. Ibid., 48–50, 52, 54, 58.

6. Ibid., 51–52.

7. Ibid., 57.

8. Ibid., 48–50, 56, 61.

9. Ibid., 50.

10. Ibid., 52.

11. Ibid.

12. Ibid., 50, 52, 55, 58.

13. Ibid., 48, 60.

There has been a tendency recently to interpret this prevalent avoidance of death as "denial," and as a denial prompted by unwarranted "fear." David Gordon's remark is typical:

> Our lives are poisoned by a fear of death. . . . Most of us are afraid to contemplate our own ending; and when anything reminds us that we too shall die, we flee and turn our thoughts to happier matters.[14]

Gordon calls for people to overcome that fear.[15]

Such an account misunderstands the situation. It supposes that death need not be denied or avoided, that it is within the sphere of human options, within the sphere to which people can variously relate through knowledge, judgment, value, and feeling. But that is precisely the supposition which the myth of extermination denies. As the abolition of the human, death simply cannot be included within the human sphere. It is the radical limit and negation of the human. It is essentially anti-human. Even the human effort to think death, to relate death to the activity of awareness must be shattered. "Avoidance" of death, therefore, is not a denial; it is the only properly human way to acknowledge the true character of death. People who want to discuss death, debate death, face death, and accept death are the deniers. They want to cover over and falsify the radical opposition to which death stands to the entire human venture. Death as extermination means that where there is death there can be no life. But it also means the reverse: where there is life—life in accord with authentic human values—there can be no death, no pursuit of death, no meditation on death, no acknowledgement of death.

3. But death cannot always be avoided. It constantly obtrudes. This requires the ethical mandate to appear in a third form: humanity must resist death actively, must keep it away as long as possible and must counteract its negating power.

Two of the major intellectual ventures in our society in the nineteenth and twentieth centuries have been responses to this form of the mandate. One has been the development of the study of history.[16] The study of history has not really been guided by the conviction that we can learn from history. On the contrary, it has shown how remarkably different the past

14. David Cole Gordon, *Overcoming the Fear of Death* (Baltimore: Penguin, 1972), 5.

15. Ibid., 14–15.

16. See "Introduction," 8 above.

has been from the present. It has rather been controlled by the desire to oppose the negating power of death. Its success means that death does not totally abolish societies and individuals from the present world. They continue to have some reality in the knowledge of the present. This aim, however, imposes a particular and inescapable demand upon the historian: he must understand the dead in terms of *their past reality*, in terms of their experience and perception of things *while they lived*. History is the effort to revive and preserve the life-experiences which death has ended.

The other major intellectual venture to oppose death has been medicine.[17] Here it is not a matter of recovering what death has already negated, but of preventing death from occurring as long as possible.

It is universally recognized that those who obey this third form of the ethical mandate cannot follow the normal way of avoidance. They must confront death in its dreadful negation and retrieve or protect life from it. The luxury of avoidance is denied them. For this calling, therefore, they require a very special equipment and must engage death with a directness which normal life should always avoid. They require a kind of special consecration.

-❧-

I take this general ethical mandate, which is imposed by the myth of extermination, as the context for the extensive death-literature of recent decades. I see that literature as reflecting two very different efforts to correct and improve this ethical mandate. They are improvements which point in opposite directions.

B. To Attain Acceptance of Death

One body of literature emphasizes the need to qualify resistance so that, without undercutting that essential posture, people may still become able and willing to accept the fact of their own deaths. This project is full of tension and instability. For it fully accepts the myth of extermination. It assumes the fact that death is nullity and oblivion, and therefore affirms the importance of resistance in all those who are loyal to the values of life. At the same time, however, it calls people to acknowledge the actuality of

17. See "Introduction," 8 above.

death, to qualify their resistance so that they are not trapped within an attitude of unrealistic "avoidance." It speaks emphatically about the need to "face the truth," not to hide from unpleasantness, not to approach life each day with a basically false sense of oneself.

But how is it possible for this view to escape an impossible conflict between the motive to affirm life by resisting extermination and the motive to accept extermination as inescapable and therefore necessary?

The most popular tactic has been to resort to the notion of death as a particular locatable event. It is something that happens at an identifiable time. This allows the following solution to the problem of motivation. As long as death is not known definitely to be imminent, people should live in resistance to it. They should struggle against it. When, however, it is established that a person has no chance of survival, then the person should discard that posture of resistance and should come to adopt a posture of acceptance.

We thus find enormous importance given to "the time of imminent dying." For this point of view it becomes crucial for medicine to be able to inform people about this time: only in this way can the postures of resistance and acceptance be prevented from getting in each other's way. Because medical specialists do have reliable (though certainly not infallible) knowledge about when a sickness or injury becomes "terminal," people are free to resist death with all their life-energies prior to that announcement by the specialists. When that announcement comes, then people are called upon to make a 180 degree reversal of attitude and to come to an acceptance of their fate.

Such an extraordinary alteration of human attitudes can hardly occur easily. Therefore a group of people are being trained whose primary task is to help people through this change, to educate those pronounced "terminally ill" into the posture of acceptance. The basic textbook of this educational effort is Elisabeth Kübler-Ross' *On Death and Dying*.[18] This seeks to provide a precise description of the emotional stages through which this reversal of attitudes requires a person to pass.

This educational effort is motivated in part by a compassion for the dying and by a desire to "make their last days more tranquil." Yet we cannot ignore the value which it has for the living. By focusing the acceptance of

18. Elisabeth Kübler-Ross, *On Death and Dying* (New York: Macmillan, 1969). Elisabeth Kübler-Ross, MD (1926–2004), was born in Zürich, Switzerland. She was a psychiatrist and author of many books including *On Death and Dying*.

death entirely within "the time of imminent dying"—with specialized personnel, case studies, and descriptions of attitudinal transformation—this enterprise has the effect of *freeing the rest of life* from the anguish of acceptance and enabling it to resist extermination with untrammeled single-mindedness. "Since you only go around once, go with gusto"[19]—until your doctor tells you the worst.

It should not be surprising that other writers have strongly rejected this solution, on the grounds that it is illusory to limit the crisis of death and the sting of truth to "the time of imminent dying." Such a perspective is criticized as being just as false as the posture of avoidance. For death, it is claimed, penetrates life *as it is being lived.* For one thing, it is simply not the case that the human consciousness can ignore this possibility until some authorized physician says, "I'm afraid I have bad news for you." From the point of view of a person in the process of living, every single moment has this possibility within it. Or more precisely, at any time when he considers the various possibilities which lie ahead of him, death is not just one of these possibilities, one eventuality alongside of others, a final event in a sequence that includes, say, getting married or taking a vacation. Death is not just a final possibility but is the all-embracing possibility. It is that possibility to which all others lead and beside which all others are relatively secondary and tenuous.

> Come now, you who say, "Today or tomorrow we will go into such and such a town and spend a year there trading and making money." Yet you have no idea what tomorrow will bring. What is your life? You are no more than a mist, seen for a little while and then dispersing. (James 4:13[20])

Consequently there is something contrived about believing that the possibility of death need only be addressed in a hospital, when we are surrounded by expert carers.

For another thing, death is present, not only as a constant possibility, but also as an ongoing experience, in the suffering of the small deaths that mark each day. Karl Rahner speaks forcefully on this matter:

19. I believe this was a commercial for Schlitz beer featuring Al Hirt (1922–1999, acclaimed New Orleans and world-wide trumpet player) sailing, fishing, hauling in a big one, and guzzling an ice cold one. The mellifluous voice of an announcer: "You only around once in life, and you gotta grab for all the gusto you can get"—meaning: drink Schlitz.

20. McGill has combined RSV and NEB translations.

. . . because we die our death in this life, because we are permanently taking leave, permanently parting, looking towards the
end, permanently disappointed, ceaselessly piercing through reali-
ties into their nothingness, continually narrowing the possibilities
of free life through our actual decisions and actual life . . . we die
throughout life . . .[21]

Far from being an objective event about which we can be forewarned by
our physicians and which we can then *at that time* be helped to accept by
our chaplains, death is ever-present. Rahner, in fact, draws a rather unexpected conclusion from these observations. The death that is dreadful is not
the final cessation of life but these dyings which we experience during our
lives. Consequently, he concludes, ". . . what we call death is really the end of
death, the death of death."[22] But apart from this conclusion the issue is clear.
The "time-of-imminent-dying" school treats a person's death as a future
fact, and therefore as something to which he can be related only through
external empirical observation, that is, only through the mediation of responsible medical knowledge. In contrast, the data which Rahner presents
mean that death is not a future event at all but a diminution of life which
every person experiences constantly and immediately. Or to put the issue
more sharply, the truth which people must accept is not the future "occur-
rence" of their death but the mortal character of their present natures. It is
themselves and not future events which is at stake.

In the light of these considerations some writers—and Martin Heidegger most influentially—have resolved the disruptive tension between
life-affirmation and death-acceptance in a very different way. They maintain that human life becomes more genuinely human, attains a higher and
richer and deeper dimension when it fully recognizes its own death.

In *Being and Time*, Heidegger recounts these enhancements.[23] For
instance, when a person recognizes that his death is his most distinctive,
most personal, most central and enveloping possibility, when he knows that

21. Karl Rahner, *On the Theology of Death*, trans. C. H. Henkey (New York: Herder
and Herder, 1965), 85. Karl Rahner (1904–1984) was a German Jesuit and one of the
great Roman Catholic Christian theologians of the twentieth century.

22. Ibid., 85.

23. Martin Heidegger, *Sein und Zeit* (Halle: Max Niemeyer, Verlag, 1941), 260ff. [Mc-
Gill's reference]. Martin Heidegger, *Being and Time*, trans. John Macquarrie and Edward
Robinson (New York: Harper & Row, 1962), 304–311. Martin Heidegger (1889–1986)
was a major modern philosopher of existential and phenomenological matters—and of
words.

by comparison with it everything else which happens to him is not really or essentially his own but is very much a matter of luck, then he will realize his essential aloneness in relation to everything else and everyone else in the world, will realize how insubstantial are all his ties with people and things. He will be enabled to see that his being is not just the product or extension of some piece of the world, some social group or natural process. He will become aware of the uniqueness and incommunicability of his own personal being. In this way, by recognizing—and living toward—death as his own essential possibility, a person is saved from falsely absolutizing some project or situation in his life which is only temporary and peripheral. He perceives its relative character, so that it loses all power to tyrannize him.

Equally important, because the possibility of his death has relativized all his other possibilities, a person is able to be free in his relations with other people. He does not have to dominate or exploit them in pursuit of his own interests, because none of his own interests are absolute for him any more. He is freed, in fact, to take (relatively) seriously the interests of other people.

Finally, and most important, the person who can take upon himself and live toward his own death is able to take authentic possession of his own existence. He is able to bear responsibility for the one he actually is. Instead of always escaping from himself with the lie that his death is only some future eventuality which he need not worry about now, he can become one with his real self. He can live with true self-possession.[24]

What has Heidegger done here? He has resolved the conflict between affirmation of life and the acceptance of death by removing the direct tension between them. The myth of extermination is usually taken to mean that life is that which death ends. Unwittingly this has the effect of defining "life" as a quantitative matter, a matter of filling time as long as possible with one's own being and activity, a matter of forestalling the events of death. Heidegger abolishes this temporal, quantitative consideration. Real life is not a matter of how long one lives but of how well one lives, of how fully and authentically one is able to live one's own life. And the significant enemy of life is not biological death but any self-alienation or self-rejection that diminishes the genuineness of personal existence. In short, Heidegger contends that life is moral and spiritual, not quantitative and physical. On that basis, he performs his one-upmanship. The death of extermination which people falsely resist for the sake of life actually functions, he claims,

24. Ibid., 26off. [McGill's reference].

as the indispensable prod and condition for true life. Extermination stands in contradiction only to life as falsely conceived, only to inauthentic life. Truly human life makes the prospect of extermination its very foundation.

However bold and invertive of ordinary perspectives, this understanding of death does not—and cannot—fully remove the conflict between life and extermination. For however much death is construed as the *source* of authentic life, this may partly counterbalance but it does not eliminate its role as the destroyer of life. The qualitatively enhanced life which death helps to establish remains subject to destruction by death. In fact, this perspective makes death's destruction seem more painful. For the more elevated a humanity which death serves to produce when in prospect, the more violating and unacceptable it appears in its negations. The fact that it is constitutive of authentic humanity seems simply to prove that it nourishes only to destroy.

C. To Purify Resistance to Death

The problem of acceptance is receiving enormous attention. There also exists a large body of literature which addresses a very different problem. For it is perfectly obvious that the myth of extermination has not yet succeeded in imposing its mandate. As the newspapers report every day, far from resisting death as an enemy, people pursue death, use death, indulge in death, and enjoy death. The myth is true and acknowledged, but somehow it fails to control human behavior. Far from worrying about why and how people should relax their resistance to death so as to be able to accept it, this literature worries about the apparent failure of resistance, the widespread complacency over death. It attacks the prevailing attitude of avoidance, not because this leaves people unprepared to face death when it comes, but because it dilutes their consciousness of death's horror and thus lessens their drive to maintain an utmost resistance to it.

A large proportion of this literature seeks to correct the situation by direct address. Paul Ramsey's essay on "The Indignity of 'Death with Dignity'" may be taken as representative of this approach. He detects in current discussions of death a tendency to view it as something "natural" and "normal," something to be comfortably integrated into our affirmation of the whole scope of existence.[25] To correct this, he reminds his readers of the uniquely incomparable value of each individual life and therefore of the

25. See Ramsey, "Indignity," 48–52.

unqualified evil of the process which obliterates that value. In other words, the basic problem, as he understands it, is that people become inattentive or forgetful of the evil of death. They may be restored to a proper sense of things by being *reminded* of true values. This strategy of reminding is very widespread today. Our society has broad tendencies to accept death, to domesticate death or to deliver death unjustifiably (war, abortion, capital punishment). The effort is made to inhibit these tendencies by recalling people to their (presumably) native sense of the sacredness of life.

Unfortunately, this reading of the situation is inadequate. The propensity to impose death and abuse death runs too deeply and persistently in human existence to be interpreted as forgetfulness and counteracted with reminders. It is not enough simply to tell people again and again that life is precious and death the enemy. There must be an analysis into the roots of this forgetfulness. What is there that induces people to fail in their resistance to death?

We may take Herbert Marcuse's *Eros and Civilization* as representative of efforts to answer this question.[26] Marcuse understands contemporary life as functioning in what he calls "a repressive civilization." People live not for the sake of gratifying their desires. They live primarily to work, which means that they postpone and repress their desires. By subjecting all persons to "the performance principle," civilization has turned people into instruments of work,[27] which channels human effort into the domination of nature and persons. Internally people have been subjected by civilization to the super-ego. Thus civilization has converted social and personal life into a "system of rewarded inhibitions,"[28] where the good is completely identified with what is socially useful. Any manifestation of pleasure for its own sake must appear as evil. If there are individuals or groups that seek gratification of the pleasure principle and thus place themselves outside the dominion of the performance principle, they challenge the very foundations of society.[29]

How are we to characterize this enormous expenditure of vital human effort for domination and inhibition, for repressing rather than gratifying

26. Herbert Marcuse, *Eros and Civilization: A Philosophical Inquiry into Freud* (London: Sphere, 1969). Herbert Marcuse (1898–1979), born in Berlin, was a philosopher, sociologist, and political theorist. He became an American citizen, teaching at Columbia, Harvard, Brandeis, and the University of California, San Diego. He was associated with the Frankfurt School and identified himself as a Marxist.

27. Ibid., 54.

28. Ibid., 73.

29. Ibid., 54.

the impulses to pleasure? According to Marcuse, what is happening here is that Eros—the basic life-energy of human existence—is being turned against itself. Borrowing a term from Freud, he says that much of the dynamic of Eros is given the form of "the death instinct."[30] He contends that our whole civilization is based entirely on the intensification and utilization of this death instinct, this turning of Eros against itself.

> The diversion of primary destructiveness from the ego to the external world feeds technological progress. . . . The death instinct is brought into the service of Eros; the aggressive impulses provide energy for the continuous alteration, mastery and exploitation of nature to the advantage of mankind. In attacking, splitting, changing, pulverizing things and animals (and, periodically, also men), man extends his dominion over the world and advances to ever richer stages of civilization.[31]

All this is in fact nothing but "socially channeled destructiveness." Marcuse quotes with approval the conclusions of Wilfred Trotter: ". . . we seem almost forced to accept the dreadful hypothesis that in the very structure and substance of all human constructive social efforts there is embodied a principle of death . . ."[32] When a civilization is constituted in this way, its "progress" can only be achieved by the release of increasingly destructive forces.[33] Marcuse constantly insists, however, that it is Eros itself which is acting in this way:

> Never before has death been so consistently taken into the essence of life; but never before also has death come so close to Eros. . . . The death instinct is destructiveness, not for its own sake, but for the relief of tension. The descent towards death is an unconscious flight from pain and want.[34]

But what of Eros' quest for gratification? Since it subjects itself to repression in all its outgoing engagements with the world, it can find full gratification only in the abolition of the world, that is, only in the nothingness of extermination. "The instinctual drive in search of ultimate and integral

---

30. Ibid.

31. Ibid., 55.

32. Ibid. See Wilfred Trotter, *Instincts of the Herd in Peace and War: 1916–1919* (London: Geoffrey Cumberlege, Oxford University Press, 1953), 196–97. Wilfred Trotter (1872–1939) was a British physician of neurosurgery.

33. Ibid., 56.

34. Ibid., 40–41.

fulfillment regresses from the pleasure principle to the Nirvana principle." Humanity has thus attained "the ultimate identity" of Eros and the death instinct, "the complete submission" of Eros to the death instinct.[35] In a repressed society, Eros can find its bliss only in death.

But there is nothing inescapably natural about this modern preoccupation with death. It is a response to particular historical conditions, viz., to the conditions of intense repression. Marcuse therefore calls for the liberation of human life from its bondage to destructive repression. This, he says, involves a two-fold move. Positively it is necessary to center our lives on the pleasure principle, on the untrammeled and unfrightened pursuit of gratification. Let Eros reign. Let Eros inform and guide reason. Let it establish morality. Let it impose those repressions which heighten its gratifications. Let it be expanded to fill the social life of whole communities.

Negatively, liberation from repression requires us to eliminate *our fear of the world*. Humanity is no longer burdened by an oppressive shortage of resources, Marcuse claims, so that the struggle for existence no longer justifies a repressive order. Nevertheless, the idea continues that humanity must struggle against the destructive power in reality itself, identified primarily with the fatality of death, and therefore must accept repression. We cannot afford to let ourselves exist for pleasure because we know that we must struggle "somewhat" against a death that finally owns us. As Marcuse sees it, the entire repressive order is now being sustained by this belief in *the ontological status of death*. Our society realizes clearly that, in order to maintain the repressive patterns on which it is based, it must perpetuate this belief. After all, society is now structured on domination and "no domination is complete without the threat of death and the recognized right to dispense death. And no domination is complete unless death, thus institutionalized, is recognized as more than a natural necessity, namely, as *justified* and as *justification*."[36]

> The cohesion of the social order depends to a considerable extent on the effectiveness with which individuals comply with death as a more than natural necessity; on their willingness, even their urge, to die many deaths which are not natural; on their agreement to sacrifice themselves and not fight death "too much." Life is not to

---

35. Ibid., 54.

36. Herbert Marcuse, "The Ideology of Death," in ed. Herman Feifel, *The Meaning of Death* (New York: McGraw-Hill, 1959), 73.

be valued too highly, at least not as the supreme good. The social
order demands compliance with toil and resignation.[37]

From this perspective many aspects of contemporary culture, which at one
level seem to function to fight death, are perceived as operating at another
level to impress people with the final and enveloping reality of death. What
else is behind the broadly felt need to restore the death penalty and thus to
reaffirm death as a social necessity? How else are we to understand the aura
of elevated mystery and power which is now associated with the medical
profession? For its self-preservation, our society knows that people must be
persuaded that it is the event of death—and not any event of or within life,
above all not pleasure—which compels our maximum reverence.

To proceed with the building of a new and non-repressive civilization,
Marcuse calls us to disabuse ourselves of the notion of fate, of the belief in
some death-giving power in the cosmos to which humanity is subject. This
represents the illegitimate "elevation of a biological fact to the dignity of an
ontological essence."[38] For Marcuse, Eros is the only ontological reality in
human existence; death is simply a biological condition of the nature *of the
individual.* Like all conditions of nature, it is something that humans may
change.

And this brings Marcuse to the final horizon of his social vision. For
he considers his whole struggle against the repressive society and against its
way of channeling Eros into death to be something only preliminary. The
aim of human existence is not to overcome this sickness. Once our lives
have escaped repression and have found their center in the pleasure principle, then we can go on to our high calling: we can focus our unrepressed
energy against death as a merely biological fact, against death as the enemy
which stands completely outside and over against our life forces.

Marcuse's whole analysis, then, is designed to purify human resistance
to death. But, he argues, to do this it is not enough to remind people of the
sanctity of life or of the unique value of the individual. We must seek to
understand why our society so fully identifies its life-energies with death.
For Marcuse the reason for this is clear: we treat extermination as a myth,
as something that rules our nature, and not as a fact. Marcuse wants to
demythologize the event of extermination. Only in this way can we abolish
the present identification of life with death and experience death as truly

37. Ibid., 74.
38. Ibid., 65.

external to our lives. Only then will it be useful simply to remind people to fight against it.

—

This schematic review of tendencies in the recent literature on death has a simple purpose: to show concretely that the myth of extermination is the universal assumption, and that that myth imposes an ethical mandate which involves several complications. The literature wrestles with these ethical problems.

I would like to challenge the myth itself.

II. Identity as Constantly Being Received

To readers of contemporary Christian theology it may come as a surprise to learn that the Christian religion is not based on the myth of extermination. Of course it is universally recognized that Christians of earlier times looked forward to "life after death." But some of the most vigorous Christian writing today invokes this myth as the primary basis for its understanding of Jesus. Specifically, it identifies the love of neighbor as the focus of Christianity and assumes that the compelling task of such love is to marshal human efforts against the threat of death.

I do not accept that perspective. As I understand the Christian religion, it rejects not only the myth of extermination, but also the principle of "the sanctity of life" which formulates the ethical mandate of that myth. In fact, as Leander Keck observes, "Jesus did not regard death as an obstacle to faith in God or as the crucial dimension about man that must be overcome."[39] In Jesus' teachings and behavior, life does not find its supreme task in resisting death, in surpassing death, or in keeping others from death. He did not call his followers to feed the poor and shelter the homeless as a defense against extermination. Keck writes:

> . . . views of death are not the source of Jesus' appeal for repentance
> and discipleship; his summons is grounded in his perception of
> the God whose kingship is actualizing itself . . . his preaching is
> not motivated by a fear of death but by a sense of his own destiny.

39. Leander E. Keck, "New Testament Views of Death" in ed. Liston O. Mills, *Perspectives on Death* (Nashville: Abingdon Press, 1969), 42. Leander E. Keck is Winkley Professor of Biblical Theology Emeritus at Yale Divinity School and former Dean of YDS.

> Death was not the central problem to be resolved. Jesus did not
> see it as his task to explain the problem of death or to overcome
> its power.[40]

My purpose is to try to explain why, in the context of Jesus, death is not *the* problem of life.

A. Ecstatic Identity

In the New Testament portrayal of Jesus, nothing is more striking than the lack of interest in Jesus' own personality. His teachings and miracles, the response of the crowds and the hostility of the authorities, his dying and his resurrection—these are not read as windows into Jesus' own experiences, feelings, insights, and growth. In other words, the center of Jesus' reality is not within Jesus himself. Everything that happens to him and is done by him—including his death—is displaced to another context and thereby reinterpreted. This portrayal, however, is understood to be a true reflection of Jesus' own way of existing. He himself did not live out of himself; he lived, so to speak, from beyond himself. In that sense he lived with an *ecstatic identity*.

In all the early testimony to Jesus, this peculiar characteristic is identified with the fact that Jesus knows that his reality is coming from God. Basic in his self-consciousness is his constant awareness of God as his Father, of God as his ongoing basis and origin. In his apprehension of God as his origin, God does not function as an external cause that once created him in the past, but as a presently and continually operative cause, as a causing.

This entails a complete reordering of the usual understanding of a person's relation to God. For this means that God does not create a person by conferring some reality to that person, by so securing him with being that he exists by virtue of the reality which God has imparted to him. For if that were the case, he would know and be himself simply by taking possession of his own reality, simply by being one with himself. What would then follow, as a second and subsequent act for him, would be his recognition that this being which he is came from God. Jesus' oddity lies in the fact that there is no moment when, to himself or before others, he is simply the reality which he possesses, simply his own self, so that a special shift of attention is necessary to be aware of God. In knowing himself, he knows

40. Ibid., 37.

the constituting activity of God as the constant and ongoing condition of his being. He never has his own being; he is continually receiving it. No reality at all is ever conferred over to him as his central being and made the content of some secure identity. He is only as one who keeps receiving himself from God. That is the ecstatic character of his identity.

This means that in the case of Jesus, and of those who are remade in his image, the normal simple sense of "I am" is altered. Normally identity is determined by drawing a boundary. Everything outside the boundary is not me, while all the content within the boundary is taken as constituting me. In other words, this simple kind of identity takes its model from material objects, specifically from the human body.

Jesus' kind of ecstatic identity shatters this simple, direct "I am." "I am" now becomes complex. I am no longer that part of reality which has been delivered over to me and now belongs stably to me. I am by virtue of a constant receiving. My "I am" exists by virtue of an activity that constantly comes from beyond itself. Relative to normal identity, such a development can only appear as a self-alienation, a self-disruption. The center within me is no longer the core of my reality; my being constantly comes from beyond me. Hence I am no longer just myself, just the being which I already have, just the being which is at my disposal. My "I am" necessarily and constantly includes God's activity of constituting me.

It often happens that the New Testament can be read without awareness of this ecstatic identity. Attention becomes focused on the claim that what Jesus brings to people is a new and exalted level of life, an existence which utterly surpasses not only the present order but also the original sinless state of Adam and Eve in paradise. He brings to them the life of God himself, "eternal life," a share in "the divine splendor." A reader can interpret this theme in a simple projective sense: here I am and the New Testament speaks of how my present self is going to be altered and improved; it reports how the self which I am within myself will be perfected, how I will "have" a life that never dies.

Such an interpretation suppresses the impact of Jesus on our reflective phase, on our sense of ourselves. In the context of Jesus, we do not start with our present selves and ask only how the selves which we now possess will be changed. We start by having to abandon and undo our present selves, by having to move toward an ecstatic, and away from a self-enclosed, identity. We have to become theocentric in our immediate self-awareness and not bring God in simply to secure and perfect the kind of being which we think we already have.

In fact, it is only the fact that God's activity is constantly constitutive of our being which allows us to believe in the exalted life. In and through Jesus, God continually constitutes us, not from ourselves, but from himself. He does not build on what we think we already are; he always begins *de novo* from himself. In short, Jesus entails a different and more exalted content to human life only because he relates that life to God in a continuing and more dynamic way. Unless a person is born over again—and born not of flesh but of the spirit—he cannot see the Kingship of God (see John 3:3–6).

In ecstatic identity, the terms of the decisive question of life are radically altered. As long as I am by virtue of the being which I possess, death is my major enemy. It abolishes all the being that is within myself. But if I am ecstatically, by virtue of God's constant gift of being, then biological death is not a decisive factor. The decisive factor can only be this: is there something which causes God to cease the giving which he establishes through Jesus Christ? That is the central and all-consuming question in the New Testament, and it is considered along two lines.

1. One possibility is that a person may act in such a way that he will alienate God and thus lose God's favor. He may fail to live by the law which constitutes God's will for humanity. In Jesus, however, the New Testament finds this possibility nullified. Jesus not only insisted that he "came for sinners," for those who found themselves in contradiction to God's will. He also was executed in a way which the Old Testament law declared to mark rejection by God (see Gal 3:13, 1 Pet 2:23f.). That Jesus rose from the dead, which is to say, that God continued to constitute Jesus after Jesus was marked with condemnation, was taken to establish that God does not withdraw his gracious giving because of sin.

Why is this so? Because law, insofar as it makes demands on us as to how we direct ourselves, defines us in terms of what we have, in terms of the energies, the intensions, the decisions and the action which are at our disposal. Law specifies a shape for the being we have. That is why Jesus' ecstatic identity excludes the law from having a central role. By Jesus we are not related to God after we manage to give proper shape to what we have; our crucial relation to God can only *precede* all our having and all our law-directed management of our having. We exist always and everywhere from God, from his constituting activity. God is the starting-point from whom we receive ourselves; he is not first the goal toward whom we reach with our self-determination. Because God constitutes us constantly from his own being, and through Jesus shares with us his life, his righteousness, his wisdom and his radiance, therefore we have no fear that sin is our given and basic reality, against which our wills must strive with the help of the law. By that sharing we are like God. Therefore (in Marcuse's terms) we are free to live directly out of the positive reality which we are immediately given and do not have to make our existence a matter of repressing and dominating and altering the reality which we find in ourselves. There is confidence in, rather than rejection of, our identities.

In the perspective of the New Testament, the crisis of accountability to God will occur at the Judgment. It is not death that constitutes the focus of dread but this Day when in view of our sin God might withdraw his nourishing activity. But in Jesus this Day has lost its dread:

> For us the perfection of [God's] love is this: that we may have confidence on the day of judgment. This we can have because even in this world [i.e., even here and now] we are as he is. There is no room for fear in love; perfect love casts out fear. For fear has to do with the pains of punishment, and anyone who is afraid has not attained the perfection of love [i.e., has not attained God's love] (1 John 4:17f.).[41]

Anyone who fears and imagines that his fate with God will be determined by how well he manages the part of reality that is at his disposal—such a person is completely out of touch with the truth about God and about himself. As disclosed in Jesus, we cannot be fearful of sin. It cannot separate us from the love of God, because, in the way in which we are constituted ecstatically, sin is not basic to us.

2. The other fearful possibility considered by the New Testament comes not from ourselves but from the world. Perhaps there is some fatality in the world, some historical agency or cosmic necessity which will disengage us from God's constituting activity, will establish itself as the source of our identity, and this will give us an identity that will be marked by loss, disintegration, and death.

In this context, the New Testament points to the sufferings and victimizations which Jesus endured. Jesus' death is now read, not as disclosing that his being is marked with God's curse, but as showing the efforts of society and of natural processes to dispose of him. His death is their effort

41. This mainly follows the NEB translation—but with differences. The brackets are McGill's.

to define his identity in their terms by proving that their rejection of him is his end. The event of resurrection is therefore taken to show that no historical force, no societal culture and no natural necessity is able to possess and to be the origin and content of human identity. Nothing can displace the constituting activity of God himself.

The resurrection means that God's constituting activity does not cease when we no longer share our received being with this world. It is not limited to the present or to the horizons of present experience. Only the being in our possession is necessarily so limited. Paul stated the situation in a striking way:

> "We are being done to death for your sake all day long," as the Scripture says. "We have been treated like sheep for slaughter." Yet, in spite of all, overwhelming victory is ours through him who loved us. For I am convinced that there is nothing in death or life, in the realm of spirits or superhuman powers, in the world as it is or as it shall be, in the forces of the universe, in heights or depths— nothing in all creation that can separate us from the love of God in Christ Jesus our Lord. (Rom 8:36–39[42])

God's constituting activity is thus taken to be totally reliable. Death as the loss of possessed being no longer means the end, no longer means extermination or debilitation or mutilation. In Jesus, God separated us from—ourselves! We are not the being that has already been conferred to us, the being which we can mismanage so as to be condemned by the law or the being which worldly forces can crush and take from us. Our identity has become ecstatic, and he from whom it constantly issues never ceases his love. His giving is not a response to our possessed reality nor in hazardous conflict with other powers: his giving issues wholly and solely out of himself, out of his free loving. That ground for identity is as inexhaustible as the being of God himself.

It should now be clear that the meaning of Jesus is not the elimination of death, but rather the reconstitution of identity such that death loses its sting [see 1 Cor 15:55]. According to one tradition, during his crucifixion Jesus said, "Father, into your hands I commit my spirit" (Luke 23:46). This cannot mean: "I have been by virtue of my own reality, but now at death, when my reality is to be taken from me, I turn to you, Father, and ask that after this dispossession you may return some kind of being to me. Into your hands I commend my spirit as a strategy for getting something

---

42. This is near to the NEB translation with minor differences.

back into my hands." This death-focused use of God does not apply. Rather "Commending myself in your hands" represents the center and heart of Jesus' identity all through his life. This is the center of his "I am." This is the structure of ecstatic identity.

B. Responsibility for What Is Received.

The constitution of human identity provides one context for the Christic reinterpretation of death. But persons do not simply receive being and energy. They also have the capacity to direct and use this being and energy. They have the capacity for self-determination and self-disposal. In the New Testament, this represents a second context for the reinterpretation of death.

It is natural today to look upon Jesus' death as some kind of disaster. Jesus was life-affirming. He called people to share and nourish each other's lives, to support and protect each other. By his dying, it is claimed, he disclosed the enormity of the evil from which he wanted humanity to turn. His dying brought into full actuality the insidious power of the killing impulse in people. It therefore establishes the urgency of his call to love.

Yet in the New Testament portrayals of Jesus, he shows no trace of this "respect for the sanctity of life," this repudiation of death. On the contrary, he is presented as *intending to die*. He means to die, he goes to Jerusalem in order to be killed. It is a process of greatest psychic anguish, as indicated by the ordeal in Gethsemane [see Matt 26:36–46, Mark 14:32–42, Luke 22:40–46]. But the presentations in the New Testament make it absolutely clear that this anguish was not an *ordeal of victimization*. Jesus' duress did not consist in the fact that he was being destroyed by external forces, by some political evil or historical condition. His anguish is portrayed primarily as a struggle within his own will: "Father, if it be your will, take this cup away from me. Yet not my will but your will be done" (Luke 22:42, NEB). His ordeal consisted in taking upon himself his imminent death, in wanting to be the one he was, viz., the one who was commissioned to die.

Therefore, there is something perverse in the tendency to look upon the crucified Jesus as a passive victim of evil. For the New Testament, his dying was seen to be the will of the Father, the prophecy of the scriptures, and a necessary element in his mission. It was indeed that which he came to want, that which he positively willed. He was "obedient unto death." The New Testament expressions are therefore emphatic: Jesus *himself* laid down his life. His life was not taken from him. This was his action. He—and not the evil of the Jews or Romans—remains always the focal agent of his dying. And he did this "for us."

New Testament writings are filled with suggestions about why Jesus died, why his dying should be beneficial to us. In connection with the present-day appeal to love as the opponent of death, I would like to emphasize a saying in the gospel of John. After announcing that the time of his death was now come, Jesus said: "In truth, in very truth I tell you that a grain of wheat remains a solitary grain unless it falls to the ground and dies; but if it dies, it bears a rich harvest" (John 12:24, NEB).[43]

To a contemporary person this image represents an astonishing proposal. For it construes death as the process of generating and communicating life. Jesus' death is related to the agricultural act of sowing. When a grain of wheat is put into the ground and cracks open, when, so to speak, it releases from itself its own life and reality, and in that sense "dies," only then does it yield a harvest. What emerges here is the principle that, within the arena of Jesus, the act of conferring and nourishing life for others requires the loss and expenditure of one's own life. The gospel of John especially celebrates Jesus' death as the process whereby the new kind of life and identity by which he was constituted was extended to the human race. His dying was the *gift* of his life to us. In that sense his death is an event of glory.

This describes the active, creative, responsible, self-determining aspect of human existence in an unexpected way. For this means that even here Jesus establishes an *ecstatic* identity. So far as he receives his being constantly from the Father, he then dispenses that being for the needs of others. In his self-determination he lives beyond himself, toward other people. His concrete actual energy, his own reality have no other shape than to be communicated to others. That communication involves loss and decisively death.

Death now appears in a new light. It is not extermination but communicating expenditure. Death is the final and inescapable mark of the communication of life. The person who loves his neighbors does not simply feel certain things. He concretely and willingly expends his aliveness for them. That is to say, he dies—if not today, then eventually. That is the inescapable truth. So far as he extends his energy, talents, and being toward the needs

---

43. As noted previously, Fyodor Dostoevsky chooses this verse as the epigraph for *The Brothers Karamazov*. McGill quotes it tirelessly.

of others, he loses something of his own reality. In the end he will lose all of his present life.

That is the truth. And in the perspective of Jesus nothing will change that truth—above all, the God and Father of Jesus will not change it. For the decisive character of Jesus' self-determination lies precisely at this point: for our ecstatic identity from God to be fulfilled, everything we have and everything we are should bear fruit in the lives of others. The only life is that which produces life in others, is the life which bears a rich harvest, is a life which becomes alive, not within the person who exercises it, but within the existence of others. He who lives only for and within himself is totally sterile and dead. Hence "the person who does not love is still in the realm of death" (1 John 3:14, NEB). That bearing fruit, that communication of our life only takes place through our losing it, through our willingly and deliberately letting go of the life that is at our disposal within us. That fatal communication is as such the decisive life-ful event, the essential meaning of our "aliveness." Our aliveness becomes alive only *ecstatically*, by passing away from us to others. He who loses his life in Jesus' name, he who lives toward others ecstatically, discovers authentic life.

Death as expenditure and communication is therefore a vital act. Jesus' crucifixion is the extension of his vitality to us, the coming into full life of his aliveness. Therefore the day of that event can only be an extraordinarily good Friday. This also means that, since Jesus' death is essentially and literally an event of our nourishment, it can only be re-presented by eating and drinking.

But how is this possible? How can anyone lay down *his own* life, the life which he himself is? What else can this be but an act of self-extermination?

Such would indeed be the case so far as any person had his being and identity in terms of his own reality, in terms of that self and vital energy which lay at his own disposal. But such is not the human condition in Jesus. Through Jesus our identity lies not within ourselves but in the constant receiving of ourselves from God. This means that we *are* not our present lives; we who are this receiving from God only "have" our present lives. We are not the same as our lives. As one who focuses his being in the constituting activity of God, a person is therefore free to let go of his life for others, not as if this were his true and only identity, his essential self, but as if this were something at his disposal, something he could really and freely use for himself or for others. The whole ethical life thus shifts its center of gravity, from how well I can nourish, sustain, and perfect the being within myself to how freely and ecstatically I communicate my being to others. "It is by this that we know what love is: that Christ laid down his life for us. And we in turn are bound to lay down our lives for our brothers" (1 John 3:16, NEB). If we see another in need, when we have enough for ourselves, and close our hearts to him, we are not living by the truth.

If this is so, we must consider a final question. Why feed the hungry and clothe the naked and shelter the homeless? Why heal the sick and visit the imprisoned? The answer is clear: not to give them bits of reality to hold on to, as if these represented the essence of their identity, but to enable them to continue to *give themselves away*. The perfection of life is to communicate life. We try to nourish the present lives which God-sustained people now "have" in order that they may continue to communicate to others, may freely continue their dying. And therefore we may bless them, not only by extending our time and energy to them in their need, but also by calling upon them to expend their time and energy for us in our need. We serve others by maintaining and empowering the lives which they presently have at their disposal. But we serve them also by letting them fructify us in our neediness. In that sense, to hide our neediness from others is just as much a violation of the Christic life as for us to keep our strengths to ourselves.

C. The "Indignity" of Death?

It should be clear how thoroughly I must oppose the basic assumptions which shape Paul Ramsey's essay on "The Indignity of 'Death with Dignity.'" Let me focus that opposition in three points.

1. The apparent value against which Ramsey measures death and the human response to death is in the unique, never-to-be-repeated value of the individual life-span. A person is exhaustively identified with the reality which he now possesses, and that reality is elevated to supreme value. The only possible ethic must therefore be the maintenance of that value. Any sense of ecstatic identity has no place at all. Neither God as the ever-active origin of a person's essential being nor death as the joyful bestowal of life upon others can have any place here. Ramsey wants death to be seen in only one perspective, as the abolition of individual life. So as not to attenuate this evil of death, he prohibits us from locating it in some larger context which might mitigate its evil. Death is nothingness. To speak, say, of death as communication would demean the precious value of this individual whom death is destroying.

2. I call this, however, only Ramsey's "apparent" primary value. For while the individual human life is primary in the order of human ends, it is death that is primary in the order of reality. Ramsey exhibits the primacy of death not only in its power to kill all individual life, but also—and perhaps equally important—in its power to make us appreciate the value of life. Without death, an individual life would be taken for granted, would be doomed to boredom. Death teaches us to value our days and be grateful.[44] Death therefore not only constitutes the primary evil and "the root of all the evil that happens under the sun,"[45] it also constitutes "the source of all human creativity."[46] This remarkable position must be named for what it is: thanatolatry. Here death steps forth as that actuality from which all good and evil flow. Is there any other way to characterize a person's god?

3. It is interesting to ask: for Ramsey where is the decisive event in which we may see the profound, the radical and all-consuming contrast between life and death? Where do we encounter death in its enormity? He answers this question explicitly: the truth about death is best revealed in the experience of the "newly dead."[47] "I suggest that there can be no gash deep enough, no physical event destructive enough to account for the felt difference between life and death that here we face."[48] In his view, then, our experience of someone who has just died opens up to us the truth that death is not simply a physical or natural event, that it is a transcendent evil, an absolute nullification of life. For Ramsey, then, the myth of extermination—as the statement of what is true for humans in the realm of all possibilities—is something we realize when we confront the newly dead. By isolating this moment from its relation to what went before and what goes after, he converts it into the event of religious revelation.

I would simply point out that the Christian burial service represents a rather different experience of the "newly dead." For in many periods,

44. See Ramsey, "Indignity," 57–58.

45. McGill is quoting from ibid., 57. See Ecclesiastes 6:1, 10:5. Ramsey's essay invests significantly in Ecclesiastes.

46. Ramsey is writing of "anxiety over death toward which we live" and refers to Reinhold Niebuhr: "That paradoxically, as Reinhold Niebuhr said, is the source of all human creativity and of all human sinfulness," 58. Reinhold Niebuhr (1892–1971) was one of great Christian thinkers of the twentieth century, Professor of Practical Theology at Union Theological Seminary in New York (1930–1960), and commentator on international politics.

47. Ibid., 59.

48. Ibid., 29.

importance has been attached to the reading of an obituary in this service. An obituary is the record of a *two-fold love*.[49]

In the life of every person there is made present what has been communicated to him by all those who have nourished him. An obituary tells of what this person has received by the expenditure of others, above all by that of his parents and family, but also by that which came from all the anonymous ones who sustained him. At the same time an obituary also records this person's life, that is, the course of his self-expenditure, *in the context of his dying*. It indicates those main arenas into which this life was slowly or quickly spilled out. In this Christic experience of the "newly dead," we do not have a theophany of the absoluteness of death. We have the integration of death with the life of giving and receiving.

In developing the perspective of the New Testament, I have not meant to find common ground with contemporary beliefs. As Leander Keck remarks in his essay, "These considerations suggest that what the New Testament says about death is grounded in a particular perspective which many people today no longer share."[50] In view of Paul Ramsey's essay, to this I can only say, Amen.[51]

---

49. See McGill, *Death and Life*, 94–95.

50. Keck, "New Testament Views of Death," 47.

51. Is McGill's treatment of Ramsey's essay appropriate to the essay's posture? Ramsey is writing mainly descriptively of the "old" death. McGill writes theologically of the "new" death. In addition to different deaths, an underlying theme in Ramsey is "the foundation of modern medicine . . ." (Ramsey, "Indignity," 54; see 55, 59–60); though McGill would have problems here as well.

IV

An Alien Good

End of the Known[1]

> Now when John heard in prison about the deeds of the Christ, he
> sent word by his disciples and said to him, "Art you he who is to
> come, or shall we look for another?" (Matt 11:2–3, RSV)

John the Baptist is the forerunner of all Israel's expectation, the figure for
Advent and the figure for us also. For us, too, Christ is always the one who
comes ever anew. Yet John is in prison, soon to be killed. But this is only
a reflection of Jesus Christ himself. Neither he who expects, nor he who
is expected are present to us apart from the strand of death. The one who
comes to meet us is the son of God [who] dies and rises for us. Our expectation, [ever?] looking forward to see the approach of Jesus Christ always
includes his death. For his death is not accidental. It is essential to the good
he brings. Our traditions affirm this in many different ways. Paul: his death
as necessary expiation of sin, to attain our reconciliation with God [see
Rom 5:10–11]. John: as corn bears fruit by dying, so life in the Son bears
fruit to us through his dying [see John 12:24].

John [falters?]: in death is the final encounter with and decisive victory over the Satanic. These are comments reflecting the fact that our eager
expectation of Jesus includes his dying. That is why the church always gathers his death into what it affirms and celebrates about him. In fact, the focus
of its celebration through bread and wine signified his death.

The authorities of Jerusalem, of course, saw it differently. For them,
subjecting Jesus to death was his negation. They assumed that his good, like
all other human goods, must [?] free of death. They had no conception that

1. No title, no date. Clearly this is an Advent sermon—penciled on eight unnumbered small sheets found in file folder #95. I have chosen the title, taking it from the text.

the death they thought they imposed on him was actually part and parcel of his bringing men into life and peace.

As believers, we can separate ourselves from the authorities in Jerusalem, but we must beware. It is just this dying aspect of Jesus Christ that also makes his coming seem like a threat, and not just a benefit. If the good and the life which he brings require his death, then this good and this life are not familiar. Death is the end of the known, the directly known. Death is the frontier of the familiar. If Jesus' death is constitutive of the good that he brings, then the good he brings is an alien good, a good located in the unknown and unfamiliar.

That, I think, is the meaning of resurrection. The resurrection does not eliminate or diminish the mystery of death. The resurrection locates the supreme good Christ brings as beyond our present horizons, as indeed the goodness proper to God. Jesus' death is the frontier of our transfiguration. Therefore, for believers Jesus' death arouses resistance. They resist the enormity, the abnormality with which death covers Jesus and his good. It makes everything about Jesus too real, too immense, too unfamiliar and unmanageable, too preposterous. All men cry out for familiar goods, for worldly reassurances, for goods not enveloped by death. Zealots want a new political order. The poor want food. The [loving?] want [services?], not laying down life.

In the four gospels, the disciples are figures of this resistance, of this protest, against Jesus' death. At Caesarea Philippi, [?] after Peter's confession of Jesus as the Christ, Jesus prophesies his death. Peter protests. Peter repudiates this element. Death is not part of the good that he expects. Jesus rebukes him: Get behind me, Satan [see Matt 16:13–23, Mark 8:27–33, Luke 9:18–22].

Upon Jesus' arrest, when Satanic death approaches, all of the disciples resist. They deny or desert him. The supreme figure of resistance is Judas. Judas' decision to go to the high priests [see Matt 26:14, Mark 14:10, Luke 22:3–4] developed in response to the stain of danger and death under which the group around Jesus was living. All four gospels relate the [act of the] woman who placed ointment on Jesus' feet [see Matt 26:6–13, Mark 14:3–9, Luke 7:36–50, John 11:2]. This is a burying gesture [see Matt 26:12, Mark 14:8]. In John's [gospel] she is identified as Mary, sister of Lazarus [see John 11:1–2], and her act represents a consent to Jesus' death. Some disciples protested, including Judas, that money [provided?] for the ointment should have been [set?] for the poor. Jesus rebuked them: the poor you will always have with you but you will not always have me [see Mathew 26:11, Mark 14:7]. This was not only a decisive statement of his death. It was also his demand that the disciples affirm him for death, as Mary has done.

Then Judas went to chief priests. Judas, too, refuses to accept Jesus' death as essential to the good which Jesus brings. But Judas turns his refusal actively against Jesus. He hands Jesus over to the forces that will kill him. If the good that Jesus brings cannot withstand death, cannot hold off death, if it requires a movement into death, then let that good be destroyed as false. It cannot be real. How can the bearer of God's life to men die? So Judas handed Jesus over to the high priest, to Pilate, and to soldiers—to death. This sequence of handing over began, however, from among the disciples, began with Judas.

As Jesus' approach to us, this Advent means our consent of his real good, to our real Lord—our consent to his death. And therefore in our lesson, Jesus says, Blessed is he who takes no offense at me [see Matt 11:6, Luke 7:23], who does not resist my death. But his death is not magical. To consent to his death means to consent to those who resisted and killed him, to fickle crowds, to Pharisees and to chief priests, to soldiers and to Pilate, and to Judas. If the good Jesus brings is alien, if his death is somehow crucial to that good, then to all this we consent.

So what we approach in this Advent is not just Christmas, Stephen's martyrdom on 26 [December, St. Stephen's Day, Feast of Stephen], Herod's killing of children on 28 [December, Holy Innocents' Day, Childermas]. That is what approaches and that is what we affirm. As Jesus' approach, Advent also means our resistance, our saying No to his death—no to Herod, no to Stephen, no to fickle crowds and to priests, to soldiers, and no to Judas. Today the form of our resistance is not denial or betrayal, but forgetfulness. We eliminate thought of Jesus' death. We abstract the joy of Christmas from his dying.

We do this, so that the goods which he brings will not be alien to us, but familiar—like all those goodies wrapped under the tree. Like the disciples, we make Advent a time to flee from his death, to look to his goods as manageable and undisturbing. Always we have this conflict between consent and resistance, between the consent of Lazarus' sister, Mary, who willingly prepared him for burial, and the resistance of Judas.

How can we not consent to his death? Is our familiar life so blessed as to be worthy of God or to be the basis for repudiating the unknown, clinging to [our] present selves? And what of those who stand visibly under the shadow of death—the aged, the sick children? Must they be excluded from this Christmas without death and the unknown it brings?[2] Must they, along with the dying Christ, be rejected from our Advent expectation?

It is a chilling thought that he who at Christmas has a reservation about Jesus, who wants something better than the Jesus who died, who wants and expects a Jesus who does not die—that such a person is already prepared to deny the real Jesus, and perhaps even, like Judas, to hand that Jesus over to destruction.

Yet, at the same time, how can we consent to his death, to any death? And seeing Christmas as the holiday for children, how can we allow it to be touched by the shadow of death? The death of children is terrible beyond words. Before their eyes and still forms, consent is dreadful. For us, the power of consent versus the power of resistance lies in Jesus himself. Against the No which Advent calls forth in us versus Judas' No and Peter's No and Herod's No, we do not set our consent, or Peter's consent, or the consent of Paul who preached nothing but Jesus Christ crucified [see 1 Cor 1:23, 2:2].

It is Jesus' own consent—his consent to the cross, his consent to the crowds, to the authorities, to Pilate, to soldiers, and to Judas. It is in Jesus' consent that we consent. Therefore we have not the good will or presumption to place Judas in our communion celebration. But Jesus does, when at the last supper he commands all the disciples, including Judas, to partake.[3]

2. But Christmas without death brings no "unknown." Advent and Christmas with death bring the unknown. So the meaning is: Must they be excluded by a Christmas without death and without the unknown which a Christmas with death brings?

3. Rowan Williams approaches this provocative theme from a different direction: "'resurrection communities', then and now, discover a gracious God in the return of Jesus to his disciples. And because such a return, of the betrayed and rejected one now clothed with power, is not self-evidently a sign of hope to the guilty, we must begin by looking closely at what the resurrection does to the idea of judgment itself: this is one obvious place where we may start to grasp why the resurrection is always gospel and never threat." Rowan Williams, *Resurrection: Interpreting the Easter Gospel* (London: Darton, Longman & Todd, 1982), 5. ". . . [T]he penitent are summoned to sit and eat at the Saviour's table, and to be themselves carriers of the gospel's judgement and the gospel's hope" (67). "Calvary is the cost of his [Jesus'] hospitality. . . ." (109).

"Hence the enormous importance of the stories of the risen Jesus breaking bread with the disciples. By their desertion, their complicity in his murder, they have ranged themselves with the lost and the guilty, they have made themselves 'marginal' to the reality of God's Kingdom. What they have to learn is that, if Jesus is indeed *wholly* given over to living and dying as 'gift,' nothing but their own hardness of heart and lack of trust can disqualify them from receiving the grace he has to give. Thus, to welcome or to be welcomed by him at a meal on the further side of Calvary is the ultimate assurance of mercy and acceptance, of indestructible love" (109). See ch. V, 98, n. 21 below. Scholar

So also it is by the power of Jesus' consent that our Advent is true, and we await the coming of the one who died unto life. It is by Jesus' consent that we move toward a real Christmas which includes the murder of children and the killing of a man like Stephen, that includes and transforms our violations of one another, indeed that sets us in a peace which passes understanding [see Phil 4:7].

We shall now do the Eucharist. I will use a simplified version from my tradition. Hymn 35.[4]

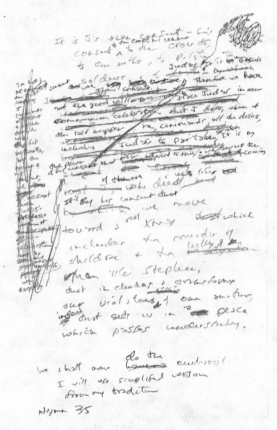

An original manuscript page in pencil with some pen additions on a 5½ by 8½ inch sheet concluding "An Alien Good" (from the last paragraph on page 77 to the end above).

---

and theologian Rowan Williams was born in Wales in 1950 and became the present Archbishop of Canterbury in 2003.

4. No reference here, but the singing of a hymn between these remarks and the Eucharist intensifies McGill's call for "consent."

V

Dying Unto Life

A New Kind of Aliveness[1]

I. *The Meaning of Jesus*: "I have come that men may have life, and
have it in all its fullness" (John 10:10, NEB).

1. Jesus is to be seen, not as a man, not as a good man, but as man expressing and embodying and bringing into fulfillment the saving action of God
for mankind.

But what is that action? What is its aim? What is God doing through
his presence in Jesus? He is gathering humanity into his own divine life.
That is, he becomes present in and through Jesus in order to be—*present!*
Not present in a static sense, as a fact may be present, but present as God,
as the source and goal and ground of all dynamic life. What he means to
accomplish by his presence is not some amazing external result, some new
product, but simply his presence, the presence of himself with and for men,
gathering them into his life.

Jesus does not tell us *about* God, does not give us truths about some
transcendent heavenly God. Jesus is himself God with us. He in his concrete historical existence, in his flesh and blood and joy and sorrow, is the
action of God where men become present in the life of God.

2. The fact that God's presence in Jesus is not only the means but also
the goal of God's purpose can be expressed in a different way.

---

1. The manuscript is untitled. I have chosen the title, taken from the essay. The section headings are McGill's. Both written and typed manuscripts exist. The file folder is
#95 marked "J's Death and Resurrection." I find no clues regarding occasion, location,
or date. Around this essay the present volume was forged with a working title of *Dying
Unto Life*.

As bearing the presence of God, God's being and life are present *to* Jesus himself. He lives in a mutual indwelling with God; he has received the divine glory. All that the Father has has been bestowed upon him, and all that he has he has offered to the Father. He is so fully enveloped and informed by God's life that he is called the Son of God.

This state is exactly God's will for mankind in their life with one another—to be his children, alive with his life, exalted by his glory, and free with his power. The good news, then, is not what Jesus is in and by himself but *how men may become what he is*, how they may share in his sonship and indwell within God's life.

The coming of Jesus—celebrated at Christmas—is therefore only the beginning of the real story. For by what right and in what way can real actual men be gathered into the new being of Jesus? These questions are settled in Jesus' death and resurrection. It is through these events, according to all the New Testament, that God's power to and in Jesus reaches beyond him to us. As a result of his death and resurrection, we become what he is. We know, from within ourselves, of the glory in which and by which he always lives. Therefore, for us to celebrate Christmas as the coming into being of our new life—our life in God—is the goal to which we are led.

3. The New Testament word for the life and glory and power of God into which the man Jesus gathers us is *love*. Love, then—or at least love as measured by this God—is essentially the act of sharing our presence, our vital creative presence with another. It is the act of *self-sharing*.

We must not therefore keep looking in the event of Jesus for things, or for kinds of love, that are not there. God's love here does not hunt up all kinds of things to satisfy people's needs. Here we receive no political program, no code for ethical behavior, no cures for diseases, no distractions from boredom. God's love works, not to make us happy, but to enable us to find happiness in the gift of his presence to us. In short, God's love is not blankly permissive, but claims us and directs us into a mutual indwelling *relationship* with him and with one another. God's love is the power of joining what is separated together, of uniting what is unlike into harmony. The union of the man Jesus into God's life and, through his death and resurrection, the union of us also into that life: this is the purpose for which Christ came. For that is the work and meaning of love: relationship, not self-satisfaction.

As the mutually shared presence of two, love for each is both an imparting of the self to the other and at the same time an ingathering of the other into the self. For so it is between the man Jesus and God, and between us and God in Jesus. Love is always and necessarily a giving and a receiving, a self-giving—giving our authentic present to the other—and a self-receiving from the other his true presence. A one-way love is utterly excluded. Teilhard de Chardin: *"Nothing is precious save what is yourself in others and others in yourself."*[2]

4. For the New Testament, Jesus brings to the world what it does not have: true life, the life of God, the life in personal relationship with God

This means that we must be prepared to be surprised in what Jesus discloses about the world, about its failures and self-deceptions. We must be ready to see normal values turned to ashes perhaps, and normally despicable things exhibited with grandeur.

II. *Death*: "My God, my God, why have you forsaken me?" (Mark 15:34).

1. The great scandal which confronts men in Jesus Christ is the reality of his death. For a person usually thinks of death as that which stands outside of life and is against life. It is usually thought therefore that life is to be perfected and enhanced by removing this alien and outside threat, by building defenses around life and killing the death-bringers: cancerous cells and bad people. As the ultimate principle and origin of life, the gods are worshiped and obeyed by people in the belief that they are themselves immune from death and can give men that immunity.

But Jesus, bearing the presence and power and glory of God, dies. He is not only overwhelmed by his enemies. He is not even able to hold the support of his followers, who betray, deny, and desert him. He is not even able to come down from the cross. What could more discredit his claims to be the bearer of life?

2. But what is this death he died? It is the *negation of life*, a real and terrible negation. The cross is no pretty picture. There death appears as something unspeakably brutal and ugly and degrading. If only Jesus had had a dramatically immense death, in a whirling fire of annihilation, in a gigantic

---

2. Pierre Teilhard de Chardin, *Hymn of the Universe*, trans. Simon Bartholomew (New York: Harper & Row, 1961), 62; italics in book. Teihard de Chardin (1881–1955) was a Jesuit priest, philosopher, paleontologist, and geologist. He is the author of *The Phenomenon of Man*.

act which would have visibly ennobled him. But death—real death—is not like that.

Death is the negation of life *from inside*. It is decay and debility. From Stephen Spender's poem "What I Expected":

What I had not foreseen
Was the gradual day
Weakening the will
Leaking the brightness away,
The lack of good to touch,
The fading of body and soul
—Smoke before wind
Corrupt, unsubstantial.

The wearing of Time,
And the watching of cripples pass
With limbs shaped like questions
In their odd twist,
The pulverous grief
Melting the bones with pity,
The sick falling from earth—
These, I could not foresee.[3]

Death is this draining away of life from within, brought on by some attack from outside, by a disease or a wound, but carrying itself through as a terrible debility. Death is wanting to be hungry but having no heart for food. Death is finding no power in oneself—or, at least, not enough power in oneself—to bear the burden of life. This is Jesus' death on the cross, this sickness, this debility, this nullity.

All pictures of Jesus as finding through his dying some enrichment of his ego, some increase in his own possessed vitality, are added later.

3. But there is another aspect of death. In every aspect of his vitality a human being must be continually nourished. For his physical life, he needs air and food. For his psychic life, he needs beauty and clarity. For his social life, he needs another to gaze at him and affirm him.

Death as the negation of life, therefore, has the character of *separation*, of being separated from the sources of nourishment. Death has often been understood in this way, as the separation of the self from the world, the

3. Stephen Spender, *Collected Poems: 1928–1953* (New York: Random House, 1934), 15–16. Stephen Spender (1909–1995) was an English poet and writer concerned especially with matters of social justice.

individual from his community, the soul from the body. Such is precisely the death of Jesus, his movement into ever-increasing, ever-deepening isolation, his separation from all sources of life.

But there is a cause of separation which gives to dying a terrible humiliation. For separation may come about, not because accidents or fate or some third party removes us from our sources of life, but because these sources themselves positively spurn and *reject us*. We are repudiated by the forces of life. *They* withdraw from us, *they* defeat us, *they* forsake and abandon us.

So it is with Jesus. Everywhere in the New Testament his death is seen as *rejection* and *abandonment*. He is rejected by his family (see Mark 3:31), by his town (see Luke 4:24), by his people, by his disciples. He knows death, not only as the separation which ends all life-giving relationships. He knows rejection and betrayal, where the life-giving relationships themselves prove to be the bearers of death. It is this rejection which is the root of humiliation, in Jesus' dying especially, but in all the little deaths that shrink our lives. To meet coldness, to meet hostility or indifference in a person to whom you say Thou is to know the humiliating side of death.

4. Such is Jesus' death, this emptying from within and this humiliating rejection from without. Yet the New Testament does not simply report how this happened to God-with-us, to the one bearing and being God's presence. It presents *his entire human life as ordained* to this death. His whole life, his whole mission, his being as the agent and revelation of God's will *is to die*! He came to die: that is the message of the New Testament.[4]

It is normal, in a secular age, to obscure this fact. The habit is to focus on some life-full acts by Jesus in his active ministry—his miracles, his kindness, his freedom, his wise sayings, etc.—to abstract these from the pattern of his whole existence, and to see the meaning of Jesus in these isolated flashes of vitality. But this contradicts the Gospel stories entirely. From the very first moment they show his life as ordained to death. From the moment of his birth when there was no room for him in the inn [see Luke 2:7] and when Mary was told how she would be pierced to the heart [see Luke 2:35], Jesus moved under the mark of rejection, and therefore toward death.

5. But what does it mean that, when in Jesus God joined himself with our life, he was immediately and, as it were, by that very fact, ordained to

---

4. He also came *to live*. The dying of self-expenditure is part of the dialectic of true life (DC).

death? It means that death does not stand outside and over against our present life. Rather death is its *essential characteristic*. Contrary to customary views, death is not external to life, is not some alien force which negates life *from outside* of life. Death is simply the outworking and necessary fruit of the kind of aliveness by which we now live. Our present normal life is not only riddled with death; it is also nourished by death. All vitality seems to require that something else or someone else be consumed and used up. And all vitality, as the enhancement of one life, seems to entail the repudiation of the life that is in others. Behind all the social games of love and kindness, the life in each self works to defend it against others and to preserve itself from others. W. H. Auden:

> Behind each sociable home-loving eye
> The private massacres are taking place;
> All Women, Jews, the Rich, the Human Race.[5]

The enemy, then, is not death, but life, or rather the kind of vitality which moves our arms and our hearts, our warriors and our priests. Death is not a private failure, an accident of collapse. Death is the mark of a corrupt life, of a deadly life.

Jesus himself insisted on this in all his teaching about "the world." The world signifies the glory and bigness and seemingly unlimited possibility of the vitality in us. The fact that when in Jesus God joined himself to our life he was immediately ordained to death means that our real enemy is the life by which we now live.

6. It has often happened that, in order to make Christ attractive to the world, the Christian church has concealed the way in which he highlights the deadly character of our present life. It rather speaks as if our life were a true and good life, and as if our death were some alien power. But to do this, it therefore must discredit and externalize our bodies. For it is in the mode of our bodies that our present vitality shows itself visibly and inescapably ordered upon death. On the one hand, the body's life requires the eating and so the killing of some living thing. On the other hand, the body's life moves to death. Thus there has always been the doctrine that man is not really a body, a mortal body. He is essentially undieable soul, to which, however, this mortal body is somehow attached.

5. W. H. Auden, "In Time of War," "A Sonnet Sequence with a verse commentary," (XIV), *The Collected Poetry of W. H. Auden* (New York: Random House, 1945), 326. Wystan Hugh Auden (1907–1973) was an English poet (who later became an American citizen) and one of the great writers of the twentieth century.

Jesus and the New Testament know nothing about an immortal soul. Man does not have his body. He is his body. His body—his *mortal* body—is an essential constituent of his deepest personhood, which is also mortal. The body does not die; the person dies. When we give our bodies to each other in love, this is the highest gift we can make. The body is not a thing. It is not "his" or "hers." It is not a dynamo of appetites nor an instrument of action and desire. In its utter nakedness it is the person—her final identity, her final sanctity and therefore her final gift. The dying of Jesus' body was the dying of him in that life which we men normally naturally have, and which he shared with us. When his body died, he himself died. When we care for each other's body, we are caring for each other's person. That is why all mere lust is built on a lie, on a contempt for the body. And that is why the doctrine of the immortality of the soul must be rejected.

7. But what does it mean that our present, normal, natural vitality is grounded on and pervaded by death? It means that that vitality does not issue from the source of all life, from God. Somewhere, somehow there has been a dislocation, a disconnection, a perversion. The deathful deadly character of life discloses a failure at the very roots of this life. This life does not grow from the unlimited aliveness of God.

That is the meaning of man's rejection of Jesus. As the bearer of the divine presence, Jesus enters our existence. And in his presence, our existence—not in its evil, degraded forms, but in its forms of high moral seriousness (the Pharisees), of profound religious dedication (the priests), and of enlightened political skill (Pilate as the representative of Roman law and government)—our existence and our vitality in these high forms rejected him, and continue to reject him.

It is rather misleading today to say that death is the wages of sin [see Rom 6:23], or to explain the disruption between our ordinary vitality and God as a matter of "sinning." Sin now means a decision of the will, which brings penalties and hurts *afterward*. Sin therefore suggests that our wills have life, but go wrong and get into trouble and produce death because we make the wrong choices with our wills. Not at all. Our willing, our wanting—like our thinking and feeling and making—is now pervaded by death. It stands on this lost side of the disruption. It cannot be appealed to as causing the disruption. There is this disruption: how or why it came about the New Testament does not say.[6]

---

6. This admission and recognition seem accurate—and momentous. We might wish McGill had lingered here—to elaborate. I am reminded of John Thiel's bold proposal:

8. Now, finally, we come to the supreme point. For Jesus was not only rejected by men. He died. When God entered the human scene, he not only generated the most intense and sweeping opposition from all the vitalities of normal life. In himself he bore the outworking of that opposition. He shared in our life, and in himself bore *the full negating force* of life.

He exposed the destructive tendencies in the ways of the world. But he did not do so as an alien critic, who watches from afar and points out the failures. He took our life, *in its negative side*, inside himself. He died. He entered the side of the men who live against God, in opposition to God, who stand with a deadly life. He who as God was rejected by men with their deadly vitality nevertheless stood within the circle of death, that is, stood as rejected by God, who is the principle of life.

And *that* was his mission: to die, to join the outcasts of this world, all those who in their vitality unwittingly reject—and are rejected by—the divine source of life. He came to bear the full and terrible weight of antagonism to God which decimates human existence. This was his mission: to descend into hell, that is, into the hell of man's opposition to God, and to take this negation upon himself.[7] Paul: "Christ was innocent of sin and yet for our sake God made him one with the sinfulness of men" (2 Cor 5:21, NEB).

Therefore, everything in the Gospel stories moves to the cross understood in this way, understood as the rejection of Jesus *by God*, understood as "My God, my God, why have you forsaken me?" [Matt 27:46, Mark 15:34]. Yet far from being abashed on this score, the New Testament witness to Jesus insists everywhere on presenting him in terms of death. As Paul summed it up: "We proclaim Christ—yes, Christ nailed to the cross" (1 Cor 1:23, NEB).

"My proposal is willing to leave the issue of death's cause behind . . . by tolerating this kind of ignorance while affirming that God does not do death, and indeed always works against it." See John E. Thiel, *God, Evil, and Innocent Suffering: A Theological Reflection* (New York: Crossroad, 2002), 173. This makes no sense in relation to McGill unless we remember that there is an old death—and a new. John E. Thiel is Professor of Religious Studies, Fairfield University, Fairfield, Connecticut.

7. See Alan E. Lewis, *Between Cross and Resurrection: A Theology of Holy Saturday* (Grand Rapids: Eerdmans, 2001). See esp. 38–40, 164, 255. Lewis references McGill appreciatively in relation to "our morbid refusal to grant death an entrance into natural life" (410, n. 4) and "the positive communication of life, through the act of giving up and self-surrender" (443, n. 46). For other references to McGill in Lewis, see 147, n. 27; 150, n. 33; 280, n. 41; 383, n. 102; 413, n. 8; 414, n. 9; 418, n. 12.

Therefore, against the Protestant tendency to portray Jesus as the healer or the teacher, as the cuddler of little children or as the friend of doughty sinners, as the opponent of all repressors or as the effeminate woe-begone one who prays, we must level an unqualified protest. Here the Roman Catholics have been correct. With their sometimes grotesque and often garish crucifixes, they have not deviated in focusing the whole of Jesus' existence in his dying.

9. The cross means that death is no accident. Death works from the very center of present life, in all its positive vitalities, because that life stands in opposition to God.

The cross means that that opposition is essential and not arbitrary. There is something essential about our normal life which makes it kill and deny life. It is not a question of God being kinder, of not taking our sins so seriously. It is a question of our securing a new life, a *new kind of aliveness*; not a new identity but a new *kind* of identity. It is therefore not a matter of God changing his attitude but of his changing the *very roots of our existence*.

The cross, therefore, means that the difficulties in our daily existence have their roots at a deeper level than we usually think. We do not get to the root of our troubles by altering a detail here or a circumstance there, by increasing the standard of living or prolonging an individual's life or securing a better distribution of food. Such efforts only give the same deadly, deathful life a new direction. They do not transfigure this life.

One thinks of the downtrodden and the outcasts. One imagines how well life and power would be used by them. For they have suffered, and therefore, we imagine, they would exercise power with their hearts in it. But in fact they too will find deadly life in themselves. They will get power, and they too will use it to feather their own nests, to indulge their lusts and advance their private interests. Heartless power is the curse of every experience of suffering; and yet those who suffer find, when they come to exercise power, the same heartlessness at the root of even their vitality. Because death and brutality have their origin at the very center of our positive vitalities, therefore Jesus did not propose some new direction for that vitality—a new political program, a new strategy for improving education—to enhance our existence.

The cross means the "transvaluation" (Friedrich Nietzsche) or the "reversal" (Karl Barth) or the "relativizing" (Paul Tillich) or the "reordering" (Karl Rahner) of all values. The God who defines all evil by his opposition to it and by his repudiation of it here in Christ takes the burden of evil upon himself, enters into the abyss of heartless powers, so that there is no negation, no evil, no brutality or hardness of heart into which men may enter unaccompanied by God. God's will to be with us and for us goes all the way, to the point of joining us where we actually are in every day of our lives: energized by the power of death—by the power of hate and fear and isolation and envy and indifference, above all by the power of indifference.

The cross therefore means that if you wish to begin to love a real person, a person who bears within himself a life-force that is, in spite of himself, inadequate and destructive, you must begin as God begins in Jesus. You must take the negatives of his life—and not just positives—inside yourself. That is called forgiveness.

III. *Resurrection as the Glory of the Cross*: The resurrected one was crucified.

1. If death were the last word about Jesus, he would prove what every human being already knows: death is law of our life. He would show that nothing—not even any so-called "God" present in him—could overcome death, could overcome the debility and rejection and heartlessness in which our daily lives are entrammeled.

But for the scriptures and the church, Jesus rose from the dead. He broke forth in glory, with that unutterable splendor that Grünewald has caught in his altar-piece[8]: ". . . he humbled himself and even accepted death—death on a cross. *Therefore* God exalted him to the heights . . ." (Phil 2:8).[9]

The resurrection, however, is not a new chapter to be added on to the story of the earthly Jesus. It changes the whole meaning of that story. For it puts the subject of that story in a new light. It means that Jesus was not dying unto death, but unto life! That in him God's humiliation on the cross was really the work of God's power and glory! That he entered into our actual life and therefore into our dying so that we might have life! That "God made him one with the sinfulness of men, so that in him we all might be made one with the goodness of God" (2 Cor 5:21, NEB).

---

8. McGill refers to the painting of the resurrection, part of the Isenheim Alterpiece (completed in 1515) of Matthias Grünewald (ca. 1470–1528) in Musée d'Unterlinden, Colmar, Alsace.

9. McGill is roughly following the NEB. He has added the italics.

Before anything can be said about the resurrected state of Jesus and the resurrection event, then, we must see how the resurrection changes the significance of Jesus' dying, how it transfigures the cross, and, since all his life was ordained to the cross, how it also alters every incident in his life.

2. The resurrection in the New Testament is not seen as a new event, a new story which begins after the earthly life of Jesus is swallowed up in negation and nullity. As a state of existence, resurrection means glory. It means the complete elimination of death, the total removal of all negation, the perfection of *aliveness*. But the point in Jesus' own history where death was defeated was not "on the third day" [Luke 24:7] when he appeared. The point where death—where the power of our present, negating heartless life—was abolished was *in his dying*. The cross was the place of decisive engagement between God and our negative destructive vitality. It was therefore the place of decisive victory—of victory not for death but for God and for life.

This is the center of the Christian religion. This gives direction to the whole Christian life. It must be grasped carefully and delicately.

3. How can Christ's death be Christ's victory? How can the humiliation of God's power in him be the vindication of God's power? How can his merciless degradation be *as such* his exaltation and coronation as the king of life? To see this, we must examine specifically in which way our present normal life stands in opposition to God, and together with that, what is the content and character of God's life as it pervades Jesus' human existence and may now be shed abroad in our hearts.

The whole earthly existence of Jesus Christ makes clear what constitutes the life and glory of God. In order to be himself most fully and truly, as he stands before us as Jesus, God does not assert himself *against* all other things, does not compel them to submission, does not dominate over them or always insist on his own way at their expense. On the contrary, this is exactly the kind of power and glory to which Jesus' whole existence is opposed. This is the power and glory sought by the world and honored by men in all their false gods.

As disclosed and made present in Jesus, God's power and majesty and glory consist in *bestowing life upon another*, in extending his being and generating beyond himself the life that is in him. The doctrine of the Trinity tries to say that this kind of power and action is the very inner reality of God. *Within himself* God is a giving, a generating, a loving. The Father *generates* the Son and gives *all that he is* to the Son: it is a total and unqualified act of self-giving. And on his part the Son *adores* the Father and gives back to the glory of the Father all that he receives. Love in this self-giving sense is therefore not one of the things God chooses to do with men, as if his identity as God, his being and life lay in some other arena, and his loving were an accidental quality which he gave to himself now and then. God's being is to love, to extend himself and to bestow himself. God does not merely have love. God *is* love.[10]

If this is the essential nature of God, in what act toward men, then, does his nature become most operative, most effectively present and therefore most manifest? In gathering men into his life, in extending his life to men. The act of God's power and glory is his giving himself to men *in their lowliness*, in their corruption, in their death. For when they are in this state, they are truly other than God and therefore, when he comes to them while they exist in this broken form, he really *comes to them*, really steps *beyond himself*, beyond the circle of his will, beyond the sphere of his life, beyond the harmony of his peace. And when he steps beyond himself to give his aliveness to us men, then—and then most truly—he is himself, the God of love.

4. What, then, is the essential and shaping characteristic of life that stands opposed to God? It is life of self-assertion and self-enclosure, a life without self-communication. It is life that grasps and possesses and holds inside itself. It is life that does not let itself go to others. Any human being who bases his identity on what he possesses, on what he is within himself, any person who is, not by virtue of the ones he or she loves, but by virtue of what belongs only to himself or herself—that person is alive with a life contrary to God. All power in this corrupt life is exercised, naturally enough, to prevent oneself being taken over and lost by the possessive energies of

---

10. See Eberhard Jüngel, *God as the Mystery of the World: On the Foundation of the Theology of the Crucified One in the Dispute between Theism and Atheism*, trans. Darrell L. Guder (Grand Rapids: Eerdmans, 1983), esp. 314–330. Jüngel's work often resonates suggestively with McGill's: "True love squanders itself. . . . when opposed by everything which is not love, it is totally unprotected and vulnerable" (325). "The death of Jesus opens a new relationship to God because it discloses the *being of God* in its *divine* vitality, on the basis of the death of Jesus. . . . God's life is compatible with the death of Jesus in that it *bears* it. . . . The doctrine of the Trinity basically has no other function than to make the story of God so true that it can be told in a responsible way" (343–344). "It was the openness for the unsurpassable nearness of God which . . . let Jesus be completely there for other people. His humanity consisted of the freedom to want to be nothing at all *for himself*. A royal freedom! And the precise opposite of moral exertion!" (358). "In love the transformation of having as man's basic attitude about himself takes place" (391). See Alan Lewis, *Between Cross and Resurrection*, 248.

others. Here integrity means withdrawal and having defenses. And here being related means using others for the expansion of oneself. It means aggression and domination. Death is the law of this life, because such life is not rooted in God's vitality. In God's power, to be is to receive and to give, to give oneself away to another and to receive *another* into oneself. Here my identity is never, never based on what I possess as my own within the circle of myself. Here my identity is based on the others who fill me with their being—"I" am really them—and on the others whom I fill with my being— "they" are really "me." Here, because life and power consist in the real conferral of one person's self to another, there can be no line drawn between me and the other. "We" is the proper pronoun—for God and for men in God's life. In giving myself to another, I have not lost myself. On the contrary, I have become myself. I have partaken of a vitality and found an identity that is grounded in God. In the words of Dag Hammarskjöld: ". . . only that can be really yours which is another's, for only what you have given, be it only in the gratitude of acceptance, is salvaged from the nothing which some day will have been your life."[11] [Once again to quote] de Chardin: "Nothing is precious save what is yourself in others and others in yourself."[12]

To live for oneself, by oneself, on the basis of what is one's own is therefore not to be alive with a vitality grounded in God. This is to be alive with a phony life, a sterile life, a life that must finally dry up from inside itself, and a life that will, in an effort to forestall its own inner drying up, work to seize nourishment from others. It is necessarily a heartless life. Therefore Jesus said, "Be on your guard against greed of every kind, for even when a man has more than enough, his wealth [that is, what he possesses as his own within and for himself][13] does not give him life" (Luke 12:15, NEB).

5. In the cross *both of these worlds* are present, one—the world of self-enclosed identity and deadly life—is passing away, while the other—the world of God's life of loving—comes into its own. Jesus' dying—not his resurrection, but his dying—is the point where death and the deadly life are defeated and abolished, and true life is enthroned.

Jesus is man gathered into God's life—not into the life of a self-enclosed, dominating, possessive God, but of a loving God who gives himself

11. Dag Hammarskjöld, *Markings*, trans. Leif Sjöberg and W. H. Auden (New York: Alfred A. Knopf, 1965), 38. Dag Hammarskjöld (1905–1961) was a distinguished Swedish statesman and diplomat. He was Secretary-General of the United Nations from 1953 until his death in a plane crash. He was awarded the Nobel Peace Prize posthumously.

12. Teilhard de Chardin, *Hymn*, 62.

13. The brackets are McGill's.

away, and whose being and power and majesty and glory lie in this giving himself away. Jesus in his manhood consents to bear the presence of God coming to us in our misery and negation, in our brutality and dying. He consents to die.

But what happened in this death? The full scope and force of destruction fell in him upon our *possessive life*, which he took into himself so that it could be abolished, so that opposition to God's life would be removed. Every bit of reality that Jesus might have claimed as his own—his followers, his influence, his body—was taken from him. His possessed reality was negated absolutely. The *deadly life* of possessiveness and self-enclosed identity—not just his deadly life but the deadly life that rules in all men—was utterly killed and abolished in him.

But Jesus in his dying—especially in his dying—shares in and bears the aliveness of God. He therefore has his other identity, his real identity, not in "this world," not in the kingdom of possessed self-enclosure which death negates, but in the Kingdom of God. That is, he has his identity, *not in what he possesses*, but *in what he receives and disperses to others*. And on the cross he disperses to others the new identity, the new vitality of living for others. As in his manhood he bears God's presence when it enters our lowliness, so also he bears God's presence as it vindicates itself in that lowliness. In his humiliation, he is exalted. The death that involved him in losing all footing within himself was the event where the true life of self-giving burst forth in him.

The cross, then, has two aspects: the destruction of the life of humanity that stands opposed to God, and the triumph of the life that belongs to God. Paul: "For in dying as he died, he died to sin, once for all, and in living as he lives, he lives to God" (Rom 6:10, NEB).

6. Here, then, in the cross as the point of transition between the "kingdom of this world" and "the Kingdom of God," we have the paradox of the Christian faith. God himself enters the realm of death—enters our realm—and in that act his identity and being as the God of bestowing love are not compromised or contradicted but established. When Jesus dies to kill the deadly kind of life, this act is itself the act of his self-giving love and is therefore, as such, his act of life. When Jesus follows his fellow men into their lowliness to liberate them from death to life, that following is Jesus' exaltation as the true bearer of God's presence. When he seems negated, then he is most fully actual. His dying for us, his emptying our present destructive life of all its power and in thus exhausting it, is the deed whereby

we live. This reconciles us to God, impoverishing the power of deadly life in us. Therefore his dying for us, expending himself for us that we may have life, is as such his act as the one irradiated by the eternal life of God.

Jesus is our Lord by the fact that he suffered under Pontius Pilate, was crucified, dead and buried, and descended into hell.[14] It was here that he found his crowning as king. His glory expressed itself in its complete lowliness. He was king and lord *in his passion and death*, and not only afterwards. Jesus attains his full power and glory *in death*! For him death is not the end but the goal, the perfection and fulfillment of his life, because for him death is the event of his self-giving to men and self-offering to his Father.

7. The outer side of the cross is sheer and total negation. Seen from the viewpoint of the deadly possessive life, Jesus is in truth wholly destroyed. But in its inner side, Jesus' act of dying is the act where deadly life is destroyed; and the life of self-expending love bursts forth as the basis of a new world.

Granted all this, granted that we must see the exaltation of Jesus in his lowliness, how is this possible? How can we look upon the cross and see victorious life? For this outer side of the cross not only conceals the inner side. It contradicts it. How can we see the No of the cross as the Yes to us of God's love and power and victory? In other words, where does the positive aliveness of Jesus as the self-expending, life-bestowing Lord burst forth where we can see it, from behind this contradictory veil of his dying?

In the resurrection! The resurrection is not his victory. It is the *manifestation*, the *expression* of the victory which he attained on the cross. In his resurrection, Jesus stands revealed as the one who was exalted *in his lowliness*!

The resurrection, then, *points backwards*. It discloses to us the glory working always in the one who from his birth moved toward rejection, negation, and death. It requires us to look again at the earthly life and death of Jesus, and see each negation, each humiliation, each dispossession which we think he suffered as something quite different: as his giving himself in obedience to the Father for the life of men. We must see these negatives as the work of his love to us, *from himself* to us, and therefore as the work of his real vitality.

---

14. See "The Apostles' Creed": "[I believe] in Jesus Christ his [God the Father's] only Son our Lord; who was conceived by the Holy Ghost, born of the Virgin Mary, suffered under Pontius Pilate, was crucified, dead, and buried; he descended into hell . . ."

Death is the end of one mode of existence. Death is communication, and therefore new existence, God's existence. Resurrection throws light backward. Resurrection is the manifestation of the victory of cross. It points backward: disclosing glory already there, the glory of life. Look again at the earthly Jesus. Loss becomes gain. Jesus for us equals his fulfillment, joy—all through his life, his losing.

Resurrection throws light forward.[15]

8. In pointing backward, the resurrection changes the meaning of our earthly existence, too. It means, in the case of Jesus, that he was living effectively, joyfully, fruitfully, and victoriously in the power of God, *not only afterwards*, when the power of death and heartless power had been abolished, but in the midst of this heartless power. When all the icy coldness of despair and hate worked upon him, just then and there the power of God was holding him, filling him, and magnifying him.

So far as men live in God's power, then, the same is true for them. They may love, may find new identities and new vitalities in loving, not in some future world, when all evil is gone, but here and now, in the midst of evil. They know, by the power of Jesus' life in them, that heartless power is not really powerful. There is only one kind of power, because there is only one God and because in Jesus God has destroyed the power which held us in opposition to him. When a man loves, because he seeks no power to enclose and reinforce himself, because he releases his vitality outward to others and willingly receives the vitality of others into himself, then he has real power and bears real fruits.

9. It is absolutely central, then, that the resurrected one be manifesting his victory on the cross. His resurrected being is not a new being, not something given to him because death destroyed all that he was before. On the contrary, his resurrected being is simply the outworking of the defeat in him of death and the complete presence of life.

But note this well. The issue therefore is not whether Jesus remained the same person from his death to his later resurrection, as if his resurrection were some new event disconnected from his death. It is on the cross that Jesus is fully alive with fully exercising God's power of self-bestowing love, even to the point of bearing in himself and there annihilating the power of deadly life. It is absolutely essential then that it is the crucified man

15. This sentence (see 97–98 below, where McGill pursues this theme) and the preceding paragraph come from a small sheet of handwritten notes attached to the typed manuscript.

who radiates glory in the resurrected state. It is the crucified body which is resurrected; it is the body which gave itself to death and which in that act was empowered by God's self-giving vitality—it is this body that shines with all trace of death removed. John Updike has a poem, "Real Easter":[16]

> Make no mistake: if He rose at all
> it was as His body;
> if the cells' dissolution did not reverse, the molecules reknit,
>   the amino acids rekindle,
> the Church will fall.
>
> It was not as the flowers,
> each soft spring recurrent;
> it was not as His Spirit in the mouths and fuddled eyes of the
>   eleven apostles;
> it was as His Flesh: ours.
>
> The same hinged thumbs and toes,
> the same valved heart
> that—pierced—died, withered, paused, and then regathered
>   out of enduring Might
> new strength to enclose.
>
> Let us not mock God with metaphor,
> analogy, sidestepping, transcendence,
> making of the event a parable, a sign painted in the faded
>   credulity of earlier ages:
> let us walk through the door.
>
> The stone is rolled back, not papier-mâché,
> not a stone in a story,
> but the vast rock of materiality that in the slow grinding of
>   time will eclipse for each of us
> the wide light of day.
>
> And if we will have an angel at the tomb,
> make it a real angel,
> weighty with Max Planck's quanta,[17] vivid with hair, opaque in

16. This is what McGill calls Updike's "Seven Stanzas at Easter." John Updike (1932–2009) was an American novelist, poet, and art and literary critic, who twice was awarded the Pulitzer Prize in Fiction.

17. Max Planck (1858–1947) was a German physicist who received the Nobel Prize in Physics in 1918.

the dawn light, robed in real linen
spun on a definite loom.

Let us not seek to make it less monstrous,
for our own convenience, our own sense of beauty,
lest, awakened in one unthinkable hour, we are embarrassed
by the miracle,
and crushed by remonstrance.[18]

10. We have been speaking here of how the resurrection points backwards, how in the resurrected Jesus what the apostles saw and what believers have seen is the glory of the crucified one, the glory of Jesus in his dying. And they have seen this because they perceive his outer dying as the event of his self-giving to us.

But where is this "to us"? Where and how are *we* included? The fact that the resurrection puts the earthly existence and death of Jesus in a new light does not explain how we who live today are involved. Whether we have a Jesus who is swallowed up in death or a Jesus who destroys the power of death in his dying, are not we still dealing with a Jesus 2000 years away from us?

The resurrection is the answer to this question. The resurrection is not just the display of the power of the power of life in Jesus, as if he were an isolated self-enclosed figure, a spectacle to be considered externally. The power in him reaches through to his disciples and to the inside of his disciples, to us and within us. The power and energy of his victory over death not only irradiates *his* being; it bursts into the lives of men. And when this power and energy of new life—of the life of self-giving love—enters inside men, it is called the Spirit.

The gift of the Spirit comes to men through the resurrected Christ, because he steps forth from behind the veil of his dying and discloses the glory by which he lived even—or rather, especially—in his dying. But what the gift of that Spirit (or power) does to us is to enable us to see the glory *in his humiliation*. We are able to look upon the cross and know from within ourselves that *that* was God's great act of power, that *there* the power of heartlessness was removed *in us* and the power of love released.

18. "Seven Stanzas as Easter," John Updike, *Collected Poems 1953–1993* (New York: Alfred A. Knopf, 1993), 20–21. McGill's rendering of the poem differs significantly from Updike's. I have made changes back to Updike. Differences in line breaks appear in different printings of the poem.

Because the power of death was overcome and Jesus rose, therefore his dying is not a deed held and enclosed within the time and the place where it occurred. The crucified one lives and reigns. The one who was dead and buried is not of the past. He did not continue to be walled within the limits of time between his birth and his death. As the crucified one, he became the Lord of all time: the power of God's love which he exercised in his dying reaches out and is able to gain authority over every moment of time, even ours.

IV. *Resurrection as the Glory of Our Future*: The crucified one rose.

1. The resurrection not only points backward, so that in his sacrificial and life-giving death Jesus stands before us Lord and King. It also points forward, to a state of existence where death—or rather, where all deadly vitality—has been abolished. It points to an existence where the aliveness of God no longer works in and under the opposing power of death, but where it shines on the surface of all things. It points to a new heaven and a new earth [see Rev 21:1].

From this perspective, the resurrected Jesus is the first appearance, the first realization of that future world.

2. But it is for us now a future world. The life of self-giving love is not to be seen vindicated on the surface of nature and history, even on the outer surface of the Christian community. How does the great apostle Paul appear outwardly? "We are weak . . . all are in disgrace . . . we go hungry and thirsty and in rags; we are roughly handled . . . They curse us . . . they persecute us . . . they slander us . . . we are treated as the excrement of the earth, the dregs of humanity" (1 Cor 4:10–13, NEB[19]). That also is how the church will and must always appear, if it is to serve its Lord, live *not* to possess and enhance itself, and *not* to serve the god of this world. But of course, under this outer form of brokenness, the self-giving power and life and joy of God is working in the community for the sake of the world. As Paul puts it, "Though our outward humanity is in decay, yet day by day we are inwardly renewed" (2 Cor 4:16, NEB).

Therefore, the condition of resurrection, the visibilizing of glory on the whole surface of our lives, is future.

3. But what does "future" mean here? It means *really beyond our view and our experience*, really inaccessible to our apprehension. Our present

19. The NEB is closest—with some modification, perhaps by McGill.

existence is still entangled in the power of death. We are directed to serve our neighbors, not in their strength and pride, but in their suffering, where heartless power seems most visible. Our minds, our beings are not yet capable of apprehending the condition of glory.

The New Testament itself is quite clear on this point. Though the apostles have not the slightest doubt that Jesus rose and that they encountered him, yet their accounts of this are incredibly vague and inadequate.[20] There are not just the glaring uncertainties about place. Did he appear in Galilee (Mark 16, Matt 28: "The disciples will see me in Galilee"), or did he appear in Jerusalem (Luke 24, Acts 1: "He told them not to leave Jerusalem"), or did he appear in both places (John 20:19, 21:1)? Even more incredible is the failure of the apostles to tell us about the risen Jesus. For consider: if you encountered someone who rose from the dead, would you spend most of your efforts telling about his birth, his working life, and his death? Wouldn't you rather take these for granted and tell everything you could about him in his resurrected state, how he looked, what he said, how you felt being with him?[21] Yet this is exactly what the New Testament does not do!

20. Consider Julian Hartt's reference to "the perceptual filling": "the question, 'What really happened?' is now understood as a variant of the question, 'What has the Lord done?' The question, 'What really happened?' is not Christianity [sic.] manageable in any other sense. . . .

"Within the boundaries of acknowledgment, the 'What really happened?' is much more concerned with the manifestation of power and authority than with the perceptual filling. The New Testament presents a uniform front on the matter of power and authority . . .

"Therefore the perceptual filling of the Resurrection is no more important for us than for Paul, no more important relative to our resurrection than to the Resurrection of Jesus Christ. The where and when in our case, relative to the perceptual order, are unavailable temporarily, to be sure; but they are also nondecisive in principle." See Julian N. Hartt, *A Christian Critique of American Culture: An Essay in Practical Theology* (New York: Harper & Row, 1967), 287.

21. Rowan Williams raises a significant consideration: ". . . the victim becomes the judge. . . . The exaltation of the condemned Jesus is presented by the disciples not as threat but as promise and hope. . . . The stress on geographical continuity in the first chapters of Acts points up the fact that the resurrection is first preached to the guilty . . . the resurrection as an invitation to *recognize one's victim as one's hope*." See Williams, *Resurrection* (New York: Pilgrim, 1984), 9, 11. This theme is woven perceptively into Williams' text: "What if the past that is returned or recovered is a record of guilt, hurt and diminution?" (32). See 48–49. The observations, 60–61, are strikingly McGillian. See also n. 3 in ch. IV above. See also Alan Lewis, *From Cross to Resurrection*, 384: "So then . . . the mutual hostility between the world and God which reigns on Easter Saturday is not the final state of their relations, but yields to affirmation, renewal, and redemption *for precisely those who secured the death of the living God . . .*" (italics added).

Why not? Because in his resurrected condition they who still live within the currents of deadly life, including the apostles, simply cannot grasp his glory in this form. They know that they encountered him, but they also know that the glory there eludes them now.

How can they grasp his glory? In what form can they, who still feel within and around themselves the currents of heartless power, apprehend his glory? The Gospels tell us. Confronted with the glory of the resurrected Jesus, and unable to grasp that glory in that form, they grasped in the form of his earthly life and his dying. They wrote of his glory, which is to say, of his expending himself for men as he did it in the midst of death. The full fruit of this glory, its bursting forth and recreating the whole surface of him—this they could not grasp, and of this they do not speak.

4. *We* actual men in our real present existence have the glory of Jesus in the form of the cross, in the form of his first coming and not in the form of his second coming. But the power of love on the cross is the power of the one and only God, is the power of the creator of heaven and earth. Therefore it cannot remain in this dying form which contradicts it. In us it cannot remain in this way. The full bursting forth of the glory of this power of love, which has occurred in Jesus, will occur in us. His glory will be ours.

V. *The Two Errors*

1. The unity of the cross and God's love is the gospel. In Jesus Christ, God's love really descends into the realm absolutely alien and hostile to him. Yet precisely there, in death, where all life and power and being is supposed to stop, he remains and vindicates himself. In Jesus Christ, he exercises his life of self-giving love in such a way that men are liberated from their deadly life and gathered into fellowship with him.

The most disastrous misunderstanding of Jesus, therefore, is that which breaks up this unity, which separates Jesus' humiliation and his exaltation. This misunderstanding constantly occurs, and it may take either of two forms.

2. The first error is to imagine that in Jesus there is a glory of life without death, that in his work and piety before his death we have the full and best manifestation in him of the power and goodness of God.

The folly here is that this tries to establish the life of God's love and glory without my decisive engagement with the negative powers in our life. It seeks to cover up and abolish the heartache and the heartlessness in us, not by coming to grips with it, but by somehow making it magically disappear. Much of the sentiments of romantic love in our time share in this error.

This error, however, is really the product of a deep despair. For every person knows that his real self and the real self of his fellow man are drenched with hostility on the one hand and impotence on the other. What, then, does it mean when men seek happiness with each other by escaping from or by ignoring this negative force? It means that they have given up the desire for *presence*, for the presence of their fellow men. It means that they want a life and a joy where their own real (and very negative) selves and the real (and very negative) selves of others are *eliminated*.

And this is emptiness! This is the emptiness at the bottom of all romantic love. It is the emptiness of abolishing real people, with their alien and twisted selves. It is wanting life on the surface, where all the depths have been eliminated, where we need not step outside ourselves into a strangeness and an otherness we cannot control.

Therefore, it is utterly without real love. Every effort by the church to show Jesus' aliveness not in his dying but elsewhere really amounts to denying that Jesus' love takes him *to us*. Rather it creates some new and glamorous world, where all negatives and therefore also all real persons evaporate.

3. The second error is to acknowledge the full reality of evil but to believe that true life and love are only possible after evil has been removed. It is to believe that the event of Jesus' death is wholly and exclusively filled with death and evil and to find the power of God only on the far side of death, that is, in the resurrection.

Thus we must oppose the excessively negative presentation of Jesus' death usually found in the stations of the cross—all those spectacles of unrelieved agony. We must oppose the whole conception of the passion story as we find it, say, in "St. Matthew's Passion" by Bach.[22] In an almost unbroken minor, it is a wonderful cloud pattern of signs and complaints and lamentations, of cries of horror and sorrow. It looks upon the cross in complete oblivion of Easter. In all that piece, Jesus never once speaks as the Victor.

As if in coming to us in our misery Jesus as such were not the power of God and glory of God. As if his coming to us, even unto death, were not his

---

22. Johann Sebastian Bach (1685–1750) wrote the *St. Matthew Passion* (*Matthäus-Passion*) in 1727.

becoming his real self as the bearer of God's love. As if this were not always the form and vindication of love.

Let me explain. I am afraid to let another inside my life, because I know myself, my ugliness, and know I will be rejected. Therefore, I always go out of myself to others. But as long as I do this, I can never know another's love; I can never know the love that comes to me. This coming of the beloved into us is what I call the *form* of love. Love always has this form, for that is when another's love counts, when, in the face of my coldness, that person does not spurn me but enters my coldness with love.

But on the other side, when we enter into another's coldness, this is not death for us. This is our becoming our real selves as sharers in the grace of God. This is our finding our authentic identities. This is our astonishing liberation. But this discovery of a new self, this liberation does not occur after we have perfected the other person[s] with our loving and removed all coldness and darkness from them. This occurs in the act of entering their coldness and bearing their self-distrust. And this is the *vindication* of love, the vindication of our experience of its power over evil.

To mourn Jesus' death as the triumph of evil is to miss the reality of love—and of God—in the most pathetic way.

VI. *The Power of the Resurrection*

By virtue of the resurrection, as the revealing of the glory of Jesus' dying, we receive *power!*—the power to love, to step beyond ourselves into another's life, and thereby to become ourselves, to find our life by losing it [see Matt 10:39, Luke 17:33]. We receive the power to make Jesus' way our own, and to step into the darkness of our neighbor's heart. This is the power to be a Christian, not merely in name and contrived behavior, but concretely in our real existence. This is the power of liberation, not yet from death, but now in the midst of death.

The key is the fact that by this power we can *bear the negatives*—no, not simply bear them, but in bearing them find and share life and joy with another.

Such power enables us to feel *gratitude*. All the goods we receive are touched by the negative; and therefore, until we can gather this negative into our joy, how can we be really grateful for the little goods, for the telephone call made in the midst of busyness?[23]

23. Let us not miss this clue to the "quotidian McGill," the concreteness McGill's

Such power enables us to know peace—not the romantic peace which seeks to evaporate all evil, but the peace of Jesus Christ, where evil is present but where its power is known and discovered to be overcome.

Such power enables us to love a neighbor who is not of "our own kind," not the repetition of our life, not the embodiment of our parents' values.

This power also enables us to unveil ourselves to another, not finally to fear our own evil, to claim another's love, not for our strengths, but for our weaknesses.

But above everything else this is the *power to pay attention* to another person. To pay attention to someone requires us to empty ourselves of other things, so nothing will get in the way of that one entering and filling us. But not to let other things fill us is to be exposed to that other.[24] It is at this critical point that love—the love for the other, the love that the other really fill us—must overcome fear [see 1 John 4:18]. Therefore, learn to pay attention. It is the hardest task. It is the most beautiful event.

The model of the power of the resurrection in all these forms is Mary. For she opened herself, against all fear, for the power of God to enter her [see Luke 1:38]. And when she bore her son, she imparted him into the darkness of human existence. She let him who was her life go to others. That was her glory. That was her love. She thus was a transmitter of life into the realm of evil.

---

theological fascinations warrant.

24. The risk is real—with the defensive, fearful shield of "other things" abandoned, vulnerability abounding. A strong strain of Buddhist compassion fills this paragraph in its invitation to "empty ourselves," which is not to say it is not also Christian.

VI

Death in Baptism and Eucharist

Identity by Having or by Expending[1]

I'm interested this evening in the phenomenon of death because it seems to me that this phenomenon has become the most intense focus of religious awareness in our day. In other words, death is seen increasingly by more and more people as the supremely sacred event. Now people show this sense of sacredness by their conviction that in the presence of death one should not laugh or chat. One should be silent in an attentive and awed reverence. No one is allowed to joke about death in our culture. It has the status which sex was given in Victorian times—it is a tabooed situation; it is too enormous, too fraught with mystery to permit our casual or manipulative speech. If our secular world has an experience of awe and reverence which compels it to silence, it is before the reality of death. The sacredness of this event, however, is not of the sort with which Christianity is familiar. It is not the sacredness of redeemed and fulfilled human existence. Just the contrary is the case.

Death is sacred as the point where human life is totally possessed by the utterly inhuman. People today betray this aspect of their awareness of death in the way in which they view and treat the dying; for they behave on the principle that death is not a human experience, a human venture. It is the cessation and obliteration of everything human. On this basis, it

1. An address given at St. John's University, Collegeville, Minnesota, July, 1970, introduced as "the third and final talk given by Dr. McGill." The title is McGill's; the subtitle is mine—taken from the text.

In brief, informal, lighthearted (and yet . . .) remarks prior to beginning his lecture, McGill says, "Now I don't know if any of you were at a liturgical demolition of the church's sacramental tradition that's been going on just after supper, and I will undertake a theological demolition of the church's sacramental tradition. So by the end of the night you ought to be pretty dechristianized."

is impossible to think significantly about death or to speak meaningfully about it. Death stands beyond the arena of humanly understandable experience. To try to bring it in terms that we can find meaningful, even to bring it into our experience as if it could be something which we take inside our awareness, something we set within the context of our other experiences—this is to misconceive its reality completely. Its power and enormity and sacredness consist precisely in its resistance to all human meanings, in its totally exceeding our ability, not only to understand it, but even to have it as an experience, and at least come to terms with it in that manner. Death is utterly sacred; it stands wholly beyond all human capacities for decision, for understanding, or for experience. To experience death is to be totally possessed by death and thus to be annihilated as a human being.

If it is impossible to think or speak significantly about death, or even to experience it humanly, then something else follows. Those who are dying are not having an experience, are not entering into a new awareness or a new realm, are not expanding their consciousness and therefore are not moving along a direction about which they can tell us and instruct us. Not at all. They can tell us nothing because death is their being nothinged. And as they approach death, they can exercise their humanity only by not looking forward to death. The entire treatment of the dying in hospitals in our country is based on this principle. No one asks them what it's like to move toward the darkness; no one awaits their words and treasures, whatever fragmentary accounts which they may give. The whole ethics of the medical profession demands that they be prevented from dying and that they not be encouraged to think about their dying and that the physician not give any hint that he wants to learn from them about dying.

The dying patient is, therefore, treated in two ways: on the one hand, he is considered as someone still in life, still human, and that means someone still primarily interested in the weather, in the ball games, in television. "Good morning, Mrs. Harrison," says the nurse, "you're looking fine today. There's some good things on television." Here the dying person is treated as human and therefore as someone quite unconnected with death.

On the other hand, he is treated as a fatally ill, as something which only machines and drugs and needles and tubes can keep alive. In one of the most grotesque details, medical treatment often finds it necessary to fill the dying person's mouth with tubes, so that he could not speak even if he wanted to. Why not?—because what is happening to him, what he is feeling and discovering about the mystery toward which he is moving, is not human, is not something we want to hear about. Here the dying person is treated as intimately connected with death and therefore as something utterly inhuman. By this same principle also, in the films and television stories, many characters are killed; but no character dies before our eyes, dies as a human being, dies speaking of this new immensity that has fallen on him. The bullet hits him, and he vanishes instantly. Killing but not dying is the human act on which we concentrate.

In our time, then, death is absolute. Death is the final immensity; and all the little gods of life, the gods that men worship in their various enterprises—art, civilization, hard work, the faith of Jesus Christ on Sunday, universal kindness and so forth—all these gods are obliterated by death. In this perspective, death is the god beyond all the other gods, the god before whom men reserve their deepest silence, their most awestruck reverence, their most rigorous taboos, and their final worship.

Now what is the Christian community doing in the face of this deep religious current of our time? I do not mean simply what doctrines, what abstract teachings does it have in its libraries. I mean in what ways does it teach Christian people to confront their own dying? How do its doctrines shape the real behavior of its members toward the dying and the event of death? Any theology of death consists only of fanciful poses unless it is tested in confrontation and gives form to real behavior.

Now what we find in Protestantism is a funeral service so thin in human richness, so clogged with nice readings we have heard before and sentimentally depressing music, so prohibitive of spontaneous feeling and creative thought and insight, that in fact it seems nothing but the extension of the hospital atmosphere—the triumph of secular despair over everything Christian.

And in Roman Catholicism we find nothing at all—there is a sacrament of extreme unction, which in the tenth and eleventh century came to be reserved for the dying but which, properly speaking, is not for the dying at all but for the sick in order that they may not die, in order that they may become well. It is not properly or essentially a sacrament whereby men may prepare to pass into death.

In short, the church seems to have nothing very significant for the event of death—at least nothing adequate to the immense religious weight which the event of death now carries for most people. And this is a shocking irresponsibility; for the center of the church's life and worship is death— the death of Jesus Christ, the cross, the event where death took not just a man but the Messiah himself, the one who bears the fullness of God's glory and power. The church nowhere can have any excuse for failing to be fully preoccupied with death. And the Christian who is inattentive to death has become unfaithful to his Lord. Because the death of Jesus is at the center of the Christian life, therefore the two chief sacraments of the church, baptism and Eucharist, are also centered in death—not in an idea of death and not in a make-believe death and not in an elsewhere death. They are centered in a real death, in our real dying. This evening I will indicate ways in which these sacraments actualize and transform death.

Now death may be considered in either of two ways. One might speak of it as the negation of life, as the draining away and deprivation of vitality. On the other hand, it may be seen as the loss of identity, as being dispossessed of whatever constitutes a person's reality. Now these two perspectives are not opposed to one another. They are two distinct ways of considering the same event. The word "identity" emphasizes that which makes something real—real to itself and real to other things. The term "life" refers to the dynamic principle by which the identity of some things consists in their movement, the movement and growth of their being from one moment into the next. Death is the stifling and cessation of that vital movement in a living creature, and for that reason it is also the end of that creature's identity. For a living creature, identity consists in having one's own vital principle within oneself; and through its life actions, its vital movements, such a creature actualizes its identity.

Now for human beings, this means that morality, the question of how to direct one's immanent vitality, involves the question of gaining a certain kind of identity. Whenever I commit myself to some action, whenever I act as myself and invest myself in some mode of behavior, my action not only produces effects out there in the world; it is also the way I express a sense of my own identity and actualize some identity for myself. In every conscious and deliberate act, a person not only exercises his vitality upon the world but also gives a shape to himself. Whatever act you choose to do also involves you in choosing a certain kind of identity for yourself.

When we look at the New Testament, we find that the writers there are very conscious of the fact that the ethical questions are really questions of life and identity. The Christian life is not to be understood as meeting a miscellaneous number of demands which God makes on them [Christians]. It is primarily a matter of one kind of life over against another kind of life, of securing one kind of identity over against another kind—the old life and the new life, the old man and the new man, the old identity and the new identity [see Rom 6:6, Eph 4:22, 24, Col 3:9–10]. That is a central preoccupation in every discussion of human behavior in the New Testament. What action you do, in that action you are not only choosing to produce certain effects and choosing to conform to certain principles. You are also choosing a kind of identity for yourself. You are exercising a certain kind of vitality.

Obviously, no understanding of death is possible in this perspective of Jesus Christ until we grasp the character of identity and of life which are disclosed there, and the loss of which would constitute death. Now on the one hand, the New Testament describes what we might describe as normal identity, as a matter of having.[2] In order to be himself and to deserve his own name, a person must possess something peculiarly and unambiguously his own. A person is real only insofar as he can draw a line around certain items: his knowledge, his talents, his body, his automobile, his reputation, and have them recognized by himself and by others as his.

In terms of this kind of identity, human vitality consists in the acquisition and maintenance of possessions, in gathering inside the circle of one's own being and control some reality. This gaining of possessions, of material or social or spiritual or moral acquisitions of his own, is not one of the things a person may or may not do. This is how a person has his reality, has his identity, exercises his aliveness. To be sure, he may wonder whether to find his identity by intellectual accomplishments or by material possessions, by writing books with his name on them or by owning a home which is legally in his name or by having a virtue which even God is compelled to reward. But the kind of identity, the manner of securing identity, is uniform in all these cases. All such conduct seeks selfhood in the same way. Of course, this sort of identity is constantly being threatened. Other people or the drift of circumstances keep working to prevent you from securing something of your own or work to dispossess you of what you already have. Someone starts a vicious rumor to destroy your good name. No publisher will accept your manuscript. At a party you are brushed aside—everyone is busy seizing possession of the space between people with their own views and never give you a chance to speak. This kind of identity, therefore, must constantly cope with this instability, must work against the possessiveness of others by vitally securing its own possessions. A person may choose to

2. The theme of having—a "technique of having," a "gospel of having"—is prominent in McGill's work. See, e.g., *Death and Life*, 14–16, 62–63. See ch. VIII below, 148–50.

withdraw from all contact as the safest move, or he may decide to move aggressively and grasp for himself as his own so much space or so many possessions or such vast knowledge or such impressive virtue that he can dominate over others and cannot be dispossessed. The life, the vital activity of people who seek this kind of identity, is necessarily preoccupied with strategies of defense and aggression.

Now if we turn to the portrayal of Jesus in the four Gospel narratives, we find there a complete rejection of this kind of identity. In his teachings and life, Jesus is set forth as one who finds his identity and exercises his aliveness in activities of self-expenditure. We have one striking portrayal of this in the parable of the Good Samaritan [Luke 10:25–37].[3] For to what goodness in the Samaritan's behavior did Jesus carefully draw our attention? One normally thinks that the primary good here must be the effects of the Samaritan's charity on the wounded man, the way in which he helped the latter to escape death, to find relief for his pain, and eventually to recover his health. Curiously enough, however, this aspect of the situation does not stand out at all. In fact, Jesus never once mentions the consequences of this service for the wounded man: whether his wounds were healed, whether he lost an eye, whether the Samaritan's charity produced a spiritual change in him, calling him perhaps to take a new and kindlier interest in his wife. What Jesus does emphasize in his narrative is not the results of the Samaritan's action but his way of acting with unlimited and single-minded self-giving. For instance, Jesus does not say that the Samaritan simply bound up the man's wounds but that he poured on them oil and wine. In describing the journey to the inn, Jesus notes that this required the Samaritan to walk since the latter apparently had only a single animal on which the wounded man had to be set [see Luke 10:34]. At the inn, Jesus stresses how the Samaritan did not go then about his own business but spent all night taking care of the man. And Jesus climaxes this portrayal with the most astonishing point of all. When in the morning the Samaritan came to settle the bill, he did not pay just for the expenses to date; he agreed to bear the full cost of any future expense that might be required for the wounded man. Take care of him, Jesus has him say to the innkeeper, and whatever more you spend, I will repay you when you come back [see Luke 10:35]. Jesus thus makes his point perfectly clear: what is good about the Samaritan is not the results of

---

3. See *Sermons of Arthur C. McGill*, 131–146. See also Marlyne Cain and David Cain, "The Risk of Hearing Death and Life in a Survivor's Story" in *Second Opinion: Health, Faith, Ethics*, vol. 20, no. 2, 26.

his love but the unqualified liberality with which he expends himself for the other's need. Now this kind of love is the constant theme of Jesus' teachings. "What shall I do to inherit eternal life?" asks the man who has fulfilled all the commandments. Go, Jesus replies, sell all that you have to feed the poor [see Matt 19:16–23, Mark 10:17–23, Luke 18:18–24]. In another context, he declares, if a man wants to sue for your shirt, let him have your coat as well. If a man in authority asks you to go one mile, go with him two. Give when you are asked to give, and do not turn your back on a man who wants to borrow [see Matt 5:40–42, Luke 6:29–30].

Now in these teachings, Jesus does not seek identity or call us to find identity by either producing good effects in other people's lives or by acquiring good things for ourselves. On the contrary, a person begins to be, as Jesus commands, only when he expends what is crucially and essentially his own for others—only when he expends himself to others. Jesus' own existence is the decisive realization of this way. From first to last, he lived a life and had an identity in self-expending service, in walking the second mile, giving everything to feed the poor, and even laying down his life for his friends [see John 15:13].

Now such is the way, as I see it, in which the question of identity is presented in the New Testament. It is not only that there are two kinds of identity. It is that these two kinds of identity are completely in contradiction. To live as Jesus claims, to turn the other cheek and walk the second mile, is utterly impractical in terms of an identity by having. If a man is ready to expend himself for others, will they not take advantage of him? Will they not soon borrow all his money and take all his clothes? Of course, says Jesus; of course, if you live in this way, you will be used up by others. Of course they will take everything you have. That is why you should expect this self-expenditure sooner or later to lead to your death, the death of your identity by possessions. But in Jesus' perspective this is exactly what is wanted; men should find their identity, their vitality, in the dynamism of self-giving and self-expenditure. No interpretation should ever be allowed to make the way of Jesus Christ practical in the logic of possessive identity. Jesus does not propose a better, a spiritual, a religious way to secure the kind of identity which we have been seeking all along. Jesus proposes a different and an utterly contrary kind of identity. To be this new man entails the failure, the collapse, the death of our old identity by possession.

Now the issue of identity put in such a radical way by the New Testament is not simply a human matter. For every person, the kind of identity he seeks will be determined by the kind of identity which he believes characterizes all reality, the kind of identity possessed by his God and established by the God he believes to rule all things. In other words, the power of identity present in Jesus is not simply a possibility of his human being. It is the disclosure of the power of identity which belongs to God. Jesus is the presence of God himself in the human scene. In him, Paul writes, the fullness of God was pleased to dwell [see Col 2:9]. Jesus' self-expending, therefore, was not a form that he put on himself to see how well it would work. It was not a technique that he was testing to see how nicely it would help him to manage his career or improve his relations with people and with God. He did not stand in the carpenter shop at Nazareth surveying various human possibilities and perhaps consulting the local library—and then came up with the decision to adopt service as his style. He was what he was solely because of what God is, for he was the presence of God in the midst of men. His walking the second mile, his giving all that he had to feed the poor, his laying down his life for his friends, were not merely human action but the actions of divinity itself. Therefore, in his self-expenditure what is being exhibited is not just the power native to human life but the power of God himself so far as men share in it. In other words, Jesus is not telling men how to reshape their lives. He is telling them what their lives become when they participate in God's own life, in what the New Testament calls eternal life, when they have the new kind of identity which God has. What their lives become is a momentum of self-expending service. Such service should be thought of, therefore, not simply as the improvement of human existence but as its transfiguration and exultation; for it is God who is self-expending love. It is God's own love that stands forth in and as Jesus Christ and that informs the loving self-expenditure of men for one another. God's love, John writes, was disclosed to us in this, that he sent his only son into the world to bring life [see John 3:16, 1 John 4:9]. God himself dwells in us if we love one another [see 1 John 4:12]. His love is brought to perfection within us.

But what of the search for the other kind of identity, identity by possession? For the New Testament writers, that, too, is seen as springing from a judgment about God. For every person who seeks to be real by securing something for himself and not by expending himself for and into others thereby declares that the ruler of reality is also one who secures and holds things for himself, who possesses and does not share. The New Testament name for God when seen in this way is Satan. Satan is the divine principle which has its own identity by possession, which wills to be worshipped for what it possesses and does not share and which requires all things to be poor and impoverished in its presence—that is, which requires no one to challenge or threaten what it possesses. In Jesus' temptations, it is the Satanic God, then, who calls upon Jesus to bow down and worship him [see Matt 4:9, Luke 4:7]. Any God who requires us to worship by bowing down, by adoring what he possesses as his own and shares with no one, is a Satanic God. The Father of Jesus Christ calls for our worship not in terms of what he possesses and we do not but in terms of what he gives to us, not in terms of how he dominates over us with a strength that only exposes our poverty but in terms of how he makes his own us, his sons, communicating to us his divine life and knowledge and power, his divine kind of identity. The worship of the Satanic God as a bowing-down is the complete contrary to the worship of the Father of Jesus Christ in the name of what he bestows. The New Testament, therefore, makes clear everywhere that, according to its understanding, a person's choice of what kind of an identity he wants is his confession of whether the Father of Jesus Christ or the Satanic rules the world. Every act we do deliberately involves us in choosing for or against an identity of self-expending service, and every choice for or against this identity is a choice for or against God, is a choice for God or for Satan.

In other words, the New Testament does not view man's predicament primarily in terms of good or bad actions. The issue of good and evil does not depend on what kind of power people exercise but on what kind of power, what kind of identity, they acknowledge as being exercised over them and their world, on what kind of power they worship as ruling their lives and their concrete situations. For this reason, the law of life in the New Testament is not that you shall do good; it is that you shall love the Lord as revealed in Jesus Christ with all your heart and soul and mind and strength [see Matt 22:37, Mark 12:30, Luke 10:27] and shall give allegiance to no form of powerfulness and no kind of identity but his. Do this and your existence must also be conformed to this kind of power and this kind of identity and will become a life of self-expending service. However, if a person submits to the Satanic realm and sees himself in a world in which fulfillment depends on the exercise of dominative power and of identity by possession, then such a person simply cannot love in the New Testament sense. It is utterly impossible for him to rest his life in the power of self-expenditure because he does not consider this to be any sort of life or identity at all.

It should be noted, incidentally, that from this perspective there is no point in leveling an attack against selfishness or in exhorting people to get busy and help others; for if a person sees himself in a world ruled by God the Father, then such a person would naturally not act selfishly. To act for another would, as such, be life for him, that is, a participation in God's kind of life. On the other hand, if a person sees himself in a kind of world where the Satanic reigns, then such a person would be insane to act unselfishly. That is why a merely ethical approach to the condition of selfishness is completely futile. In a world of cancer and bombs, where weakness brings contempt and insignificance brings loneliness, it would monstrous to be unselfish. Consequently, whether people serve themselves or serve others, whether they find identity by having or by expending, is not in their power to choose. This is decided only in terms of the kind of world in which they think they live, in terms of the kind of power which they see ruling the roost. The issue lies at the level of the God they worship and not in the kind of person they want to be. In New Testament terms, they live or die according to the king that holds them and the kingdom to which they belong.

The event of becoming a Christian, of confessing that Jesus Christ is Lord, involves a person being grounded in, in taking on, Jesus' kind of identity. The sacrament of baptism is the actualization of this event. What does it mean to be grounded in, to take on, Jesus' kind of identity? Here is the first and, in a sense, the most crucial point in the entire discussion. The very peculiar New Testament perspective on this point might be formulated in this way: it is in Jesus that a person is grounded in and takes on Jesus' kind of identity. It is in the events of God's action in Jesus of Nazareth at the beginning of our era, it is in those actions away over there and away back then that any individual secures the kind of identity which God has. In other words, then, in order to secure this new kind of identity, I cannot acquire it in myself as I live here and now. I must be carried back into Jesus Christ, into the events which constitute his being. It is not that he comes to me and causes things to happen in me. It is not that I, existing wholly within the circle of my present world, somehow manage to receive the new identity of Jesus, somehow become the new being and then turn to Jesus as he is presented in the New Testament and the worship of the church. It is rather that in order to receive this new identity, I must be taken out the present world and out of the identity which my present world gives me. This is the meaning and the necessity of baptism. It is the means through which the circle of my existence is broken open. I cease to see myself and know myself in terms of my immediately visible environment. I begin to see and know myself as *in* Jesus Christ. My identity is to be received by being gathered into the life he lived, and baptism draws me into his life.

We must understand clearly what this entails. In this view, baptism does not express to the world what has happened to me within my own being, in my mind by some spiritual and invisible influence of God. At the same time, baptism as an action does not itself produce any effects on me, except one. It relates me in my self-understanding to Jesus Christ. It causes me to seek my identity not in myself and not even in myself as affected by the church or by the people or by books or by God, but to seek my identity in him, in what he did, in what he was, in what he went through.

That is how I would understand the old principle that baptism, like all the sacraments, is an effective sign. It is not a thing which produces effects, like magical water or gamma radiation; it is a sign. When it occurs, it presents us with something other than itself, something absent from our immediate surroundings, something not otherwise available. It presents us with Jesus Christ as the place for our securing our identity. It is only a sign. But it is a sign which bears on our sense of our identities, and therein lies its effectiveness. It is effective as a sign in its power to signify. Its effectiveness does not refer to after effects it produces, as if it were a physical cause that produces effects. Its effectiveness refers to its signifying. It signifies the absent, the back-there reality of Jesus Christ; and it does so with such power that my sense of myself, my existence as a vitally conscious self, finds itself taken into Jesus. To use the phrases of Paul, I become united to Christ [see Rom 6:5, Eph 4:13]. I now live in Jesus Christ [see Gal 2:20, 2 Tim 3:12]. That is, I now exercise a vitality and stand on an identity which is not grounded in myself but which is in him, which I find always in him and never merely in myself, but which, when I find it in him, really and effectively is the basis for my vitality and my identity. The effectiveness of baptism as a sign means that it doesn't stand there; it disappears, so to speak, in a way that a clean window disappears from sight. When I participate in baptism, I am led through it to Jesus. Jesus is the effective one and not baptism. Baptism is effective only in the sense of being so fully a sign, so perfectly transparent, that it no longer stands in the way between myself and Jesus. It is not another event in my immediate experience which holds me into myself and only has value insofar as it gives me something inside the circle of what is my own. Baptism shatters once and for all the closed circle of my living by what is my own.

But now we must turn to the next question. Granted that baptism becomes really transparent of Jesus, so that in the form of the baptismal event I am in Jesus and there in him receive my new identity. Granted all this, what happens to me? What do I go through when I am there in Jesus? The answer is obvious. I have my old identity taken from me and a new kind of identity given me. I do not lose my old identity in myself, here and now in my present world, and then go to Jesus by a baptism for my new identity. I am taken to Jesus by a baptism and there in him both lose my old possessive kind of identity and gain my new one. Paul speaks of this in Romans 6:3 [-4, NEB]: "Have you forgotten that when we were baptized into union with Christ Jesus, we were baptized into his death? By baptism we were buried with him and laid dead, in order that, as Jesus Christ was raised from the dead in the splendor of the Father, so also we might set our feet upon the new path of life." In short, according to Paul, I lose my old kind of identity in being united with Christ in his dying so that I may then secure the new identity through Christ's resurrection.

Now the point which I believe must be emphasized here in our day is this dying with Christ, this share which we have in his death, this loss of our old identity. We can speak of this dying in two ways. First, from the objective side, in terms of what is being done to us, we might say this destruction of us with our old identity is God's judgment upon our life of sin. Here, because this takes place in Jesus Christ, there is acting the same action involved in Jesus' death, the action of God in putting to death the power of evil, the purifying judgment of God by which we die in our evil existence so that we might rise to new life and new identity. God's judgment is how we are justified, how we are made righteous and pleasing to God. The new man is born only after the old man dies; and both events happen for us in Jesus Christ and therefore are God's doing, our death being his judgment and our rising to new life being his justification of us. God's judgment upon us is the work of his love since it takes place in Jesus Christ, whose death was for the sake of our glorification.

Now the fact that this dying must be God's act constitutes a very important principle; for what is involved is not the removal from us of our identity and its replacement with another, as if the identities here were some kind of surface garments. What is involved is the removal of *my* identity, my real identity, the only kind of identity I have ever known. It involves my death: the real killing and obliterating of the *me* who has found its whole and only actuality in a kind of vitality and identity which are now being destroyed. It is not enough, therefore, to say that my identity is removed. We must say, I die. I am killed. I lose the identity in life that is identical to my reality up to this point. That is why it is only God who can act here. No other reality can kill us deeply enough, can reach far enough down to the very roots of our old life, our old possessive identity. Therefore, neither the death which I might give myself or which my neighbors or my enemies may give me or which diseases or accidents may give me, goes deeply enough.

God does execute upon me this act of radical killing, but he does not execute it upon me in myself. He executes it in Jesus Christ, in the death of Jesus, where our manhood is radically uprooted and the new life bestowed. This is how I would understand the Christian prohibition against suicide and murder. It is *not* that killing is wrong and that the life we now live, this possessive, defensive, aggressive existence, is sacred; on the contrary, killing is what we need, the killing of a deeply perverse vitality. The trouble is no murder and no suicide can be radical enough; and if Jesus' death were only a matter of the heart stopping and people being cruel, if his death did not involve a breaking by God, the exercise of God's negating judgment against evil, then Jesus' death would not lead to any newness of life. It would be a surface death, leaving the old man, the old identity, which would rise again to the old life. If I try to kill myself, that is an act of my old identity. The I that is doing the suicide is not really different from the me and the life that I am thus seeking to escape.

The impulse to suicide is true and right. It is grounded in the perception that my identity in the circle of my circumstances is a dreadful identity. But no man can execute upon himself a death thorough enough and total enough to redeem him from his old identity. He cannot inflict upon himself a suicide that is suicidal enough to fulfill this impulse, nor can we inflict this upon each other. If we rise to newness of life, it is because we die by God's saving action; it is because we die in Jesus Christ and with Jesus Christ.

Let us now notice what this dying with Christ means, not objectively, in terms of what is being done to us, but subjectively, in terms of what we experience. One decisive and inescapable emotion is obvious. There *is* terror—to enter baptism, which is not a bit of ecclesiastical business but which is a sign that enables us to perceive ourselves in Christ—to enter baptism is to die, to find oneself [ourselves] in a perspective, in a situation where we are deprived of the only kind of identity, the only kind of life we have ever known. We find our whole existence of having being negated. All the identity we have secured by acquiring knowledge, by acquiring virtue, by acquiring children, by acquiring friends—I am utterly and totally dispossessed, and in the grip of an energy so dispossessing that Jesus Christ hanging naked on the cross is its full execution. There is this terrific negative emotion.

Yet there is something else. There is the deep inner *consent* to this death, a consent which wrestles against this terror and overcomes it. The premise of baptism, and we cannot possibly minimize this, the premise of baptism is our willingness, our deep wanting to die with Christ, to be killed with him in the only identity we have known, to take into ourselves the judgment of God. Do you want newness of life? You cannot possibly have it unless you are willing to consent to a death which plunges deeper into your being than any disease or murder or natural dying. For if you are not willing to do this, then you do not understand what Jesus Christ has for you. You imagine that he has some satisfaction for your old self, some new and better possession which you can take within the circle of yourself. You think that you can receive what he has for you without dying. You are wrong. He has for you life with a new God, and therefore a radically new kind of life, an identity in and as self-giving, an identity by expending toward others of everything which you receive. If you do not want this, baptism is beside the point.

Now the New Testament has a very special name for this willingness to die with Christ, this consent to which holds in check that terror that makes us want to hold onto our old identity. And the New Testament name for this willingness is faith. Baptism, then, requires our consent to die with Christ, so that we might rise to newness of life. Baptism is our union with Christ dying so that we might rise with him. But the event of baptism does not complete the end of the old man in us. It is our union with Christ, our entering with him into judgment, the beginning of our faith. But as Paul puts it so vividly, our whole life, as long as we live in the present world, involves the continual dying of the old man in us and the continual growing in us of the new man who lives for God [see Rom 6:5–11].

Baptism is an initiation into tension. It is not a transformation into glory. The baptized Christian anew each day discovers the power of the old man still within him which he submits to and which he finds gathered into the death of Christ. He continues to need judgment all the rest of his days, and the newness of life is not something which becomes implanted naturally in him by baptism. He lives toward the new life and strains for it continually. Therefore, on his last day, the Christian finds himself just where he was at baptism. He finds that he is going to lose his identity by possession, his worldly identity. People will bury him and forget him. He will not be as body and so not be. He again confronts the crisis of dispossession. But not for the first time. What he confronts at his death bed, the terror of letting go to what he has been given, the necessity to consent to the death of this kind of identity that he may be [living?] of God and for God, this terror and this consent has been his practice from the day of his baptism. And because of his baptism, because he is united in Christ's death, therefore in this final deprivation, he does not simply die within himself; and he does not die simply through the inadequate action of diseases or injury or physiological breakdown. This, too, is gathered into Christ's crucifixion. So far as he still resists dying, so far as he feels terror at the loss of his old identity, of his identity as the world knows it, he is to be reminded of his baptismal promise. His faith is to be encouraged, and he is to move against this terror with his eagerness for the perfection of his new identity in Jesus Christ. He is to consent to dying and to letting his body feed the ground. The church has only one service that is connected with the death that terrifies us, and that is the service of baptism.[4]

One of the unexpected consequences of these reflections is in my growing conviction that the present ritual of baptism in our churches does not make clear and central the presence of death. For one thing, there is no

---

4. In detached notes accompanying this lecture, we find: "Cyril Myst Lect I.3 Pharoah drowned in Red Sea, so devil drowned in baptism." See Cyril of Jerusalem, "Five Catechetical Lectures of the Same Author, to The Newly Baptized. Lecture XIX. First Lecture on the Mysteries." "The tyrant of old was drowned in the sea; and this present one disappears in the water of salvation." And this note: "Cyril says that the threefold immersion (Myst on Baptism Lect II.4) had reference to the three days of our Lord's burial." See Cyril, "Lecture XX. (On the Mysteries, II.) Of Baptism." "And each of you was asked, whether he believed in the name of the Father, and of the Son, and of the Holy Ghost, and ye made that saving confession, and descended three times into the water, and ascended again; here also hinting by a symbol at the three-days burial of Christ. For as our Saviour passed three days and three nights in the heart of the earth, so you also in your first ascent out of the water, represented the first day of Christ in the earth, and by your descent, the night; for as he who is in the night, no longer sees, but he who is in the day, remains in the light, so in the descent, as in the night, ye saw nothing, but in ascending again ye were in the day. And at the self-same moment ye were as in the day. And at the self-same moment ye were both dying and being born; and that Water of salvation was at once your grave and your mother." See *A Select Library of Nicene and Post-Nicene Fathers of the Christian Church*, Second Series, eds. Henry Wace and Philip Schaff, (Oxford: James Parker and Company, 1894), vol. VII, S. Cyril of Jerusalem: Catechetical Lectures, 145, 147–148. St. Cyril of Jerusalem (ca. 313–386), Archbishop of Jerusalem from about 350, delivered his twenty-three "Catechetical Lectures" about 347–348.

immersion, no going down into the water. But more serious, I am beginning to think, is the fact of infant baptism. I am not against infant baptism, but I find that I am against the meaning which infant baptism gives to the sacrament. For the presence of the infant excludes, not only the dying element, but the agonized consent to dying.

Four things happen, it seems to me, when infant baptism is the normal thing. First, the precondition of faith as one's consent to losing one's old identity disappears. Faith comes to be seen as something else, something more amenable to infants, some assurance that is not in terrible tension with terror, but something which a whole community can complacently believe. Faith, the faith which the Christian carries each day, ceases to be the consent to submit to God's judgment.

Secondly, infant baptism encourages a misunderstanding about God. Because an infant can't as such be joined to Christ, then obviously God is not executing any judgment in the process upon infants, inside the infant. What, then, happens to God's judgment, God's judging action? It becomes not something to which every Christian constantly submits himself as the essential element in his liberation to new life. Not at all. God's judgment becomes something reserved exclusively for those whom God condemns. It becomes separated from God's love so that if God is pleased for his infant child, he baptizes and so forth. But those he is against he smashes to pieces in endless torment. Because of infant baptism the church was forced either in two directions. God does condemn, said some, but his condemnation is not for the sake of healing men; it is an alternative to his healing men. Others said that God is love and so there is no judgment, no condemnation at all. The entire theology of God's judgment becomes falsified when infant baptism conceals from us all the fact that there is no joining to Christ as new life except by the deepest and most difficult dying with him to our old selves by the execution upon us of God's judgment which is the act of his love.

Third, infant baptism helps create the impression that the Christian life is a matter of growing up, a simple, almost natural process of letting the new life in us bear fruit. There is no suggestion of the tension in the Christian life, of living with the old man dying each day and the new man growing. Therefore, it was to be expected that baptized Christianity came to be looked upon as a pretty poor and second-rate affair. True, full Christian existence was a matter of this dying and rising, this incredible tension; and this was the vocation of those in the monastic orders. It was only right, therefore, for them to reject their baptized names when they entered this life because baptism as practiced, infant baptism, represents a childish and immature relation to Jesus.

Fourth and finally, the practice of infant baptism so obscured the present of our dying at the center of this ritual that our dying became an event that seemed never to be directly addressed by the church. The ointment for the sick was called to fill the gap, but that was weak. In other words, one important source for the church's irresponsibility toward death in our day has been its clinging to the infant conception of baptism.

When we turn to the Eucharist, we are turning to the feast of life, to the feast of our nourishment. What does Christ's death mean in this context? And the answer is obvious. Christ's death is that losing of his life that it might pass into us. Now the Gospel of John is built on this basis. He presents the incarnation as the union of Jesus' humanity with God, as the creation of a new humanity united with and in the divine life. The Father is in me and I am in the Father, says the new man Jesus [see John 14:10]. The humanity of Jesus is therefore full of life—full of its own activity, namely the activity of offering himself to the Father, of glorifying the Father and doing the Father's will. If the Father dwells in the new humanity of Jesus, the new humanity of Jesus dwells in the Father; and this mutual indwelling is in the Gospel of John called love.

Where does Jesus make visible his life, his activity of offering glory to the Father, of giving up all he has to the Father's glory? He does this in his death. His death on the cross is the manifestation of his life. It appears as death only to Satanic eyes that judge in terms of possessed identity. But here on the cross, the integrity and the totality with which Jesus lives out of himself toward God, lives for God and dynamically into God and not for himself and not claustrophobically within himself, becomes manifest. When I am raised up, by which he meant upon the cross, then shall the Father be glorified and I shall draw all men to myself [see John 12:32]. Here on the cross the new humanity offers all, offers its very life to the Father. But that offering is its vital principle, is the essence of its new kind of aliveness, is the essence of its aliveness in the life of God.

How can that new humanity be ours? Only if it is broken up so that we may take it in. And this is John's theme of eating and drinking the new humanity of Christ. The Eucharist is the actualization by which Christ's humanity in its supremely vital act, its offering to the Father on the cross, is imparted to us. You must eat his flesh and you must drink his blood [see

John 6:53–58]. Why is Christ's body broken? Not to kill it but to scatter it so that we may receive it. Why is his blood poured out? Not so that he may die. It is poured out for us to drink.

There is no death here. We have been wrong in trying to interpret the meal as if it represented Christ's death, the death of the old man. We must not interpret the meal as if it were a death. We must interpret the death as a meal, as his way of extending himself to us and nourishing us with his vitality of offering himself to the Father. The Eucharist is not baptism, is not a participation in the judgment of death. The Eucharist is only possible for those who have already given up their old identity, their search for their old identity, and their life toward a God who will confirm them in their old identity. The Eucharist is feast and fullness. It is a participation in Christ's self-offering to the Father; it is a participation in the fullness of life. And because we participate by taking him into ourselves we must not just consent but rejoice in eating him. If in death we consented to the killing of our old selves, in the Eucharist we consent to a death that is no death at all but the extension of life. We must take him into ourselves that we may be gathered into his giving to the Father.

Death here has lost its sting [see 1 Cor 15:55]. Death here is not death. It is the letting go which is life. Here we consent to the death of Jesus with joy, for it is always his aliveness and not his death. Here is the anticipation of the new heaven and the new earth [see Rev 21:1] where every tear is washed away [see Rev 21:4]. Here the power of letting go is experienced as nourishing. Thank you.

-●-

[In the question-response discussion following this lecture, one "question" is a comment to the effect that there is nothing theologically prohibiting infant baptism. Here is McGill's response.]

Well, it's only a kind of small step for me to take. It certainly prohibits the normal infant baptism but under abnormal circumstances might be legitimate. But normally to expect that the way most humans will become identified with Jesus will be before they will have their old identity and are self-conscious about their old identity and are called therefore to let go of their old identity and to immerse themselves into the water and come out again. No. I'd say when this [letting go of their old identity, dying and rising] becomes abnormal, then the church has forgotten the meaning of baptism.

[There is further discussion as the questioner wonders about the relationship between the individual being baptized and the church community.]

There's no way—it's inconceivable to me that an adult being baptized, that because it's his experience it's therefore cut off from the community. No, I mean he's got the experience of dying and in that he is conscious that he is participating in the experience the community has experienced. The principle that there should be a non-experiencer is the principle of infant baptism, that the community replaces the subject's experience, and this a very astonishing position—in abnormal circumstances possible. But as a sort of normal thing that there's a non-experiencer here: this says something, something I think very pernicious about the way God is related to us.

Now let me tell you how Protestant and Catholic theologians talk when they defend infant baptism. They say that it is a sign—and this has always been my position until recently—infant baptism is the sign that we do nothing, and it is God's pure gift. And this is what we're all intended to believe. Now the implication of this way of conceiving of how I must be when God acts is to say in order for it to be God's act, I must be inhuman. In order for God to act, I must not act. Now there's nothing like that in the New Testament, no intimation that the condition for God to act is for me not to act. On the contrary, the condition for God's action is to call me into action. It isn't that I have to cut everything off, and then God gets a chance. God's action doesn't require the suppression of human action.

Therefore, one of the things that infant baptism tends to suggest is that the basis for our life in God is a kind of neutral condition, a kind of unbeing, just an emptiness. And then God comes in. But you see this is exactly what the New Testament denies. It is not the case that I become a Christian by sort of being empty and then becoming full. That is not what it is. Rather, I am full of what is wrong, and this must be killed. Therefore, the image of the infant is, it seems to me, a lie. That is not the image we should have for what it means to become a Christian, to sort of be empty and into the emptiness God acts. No.

What God acts upon is not an emptiness but something we are and *will* to be. So that the meaning of baptism is the consent to let go of what we are. And if normally this is eliminated and further eliminated in a way that is better for God if we're not acting at all and our old man isn't there yet and is just the nice child, you know, virginal and sort of neutral—then what we're really saying is God's judgment isn't the way we're healed. We're healed only from vacuity—the infant. And God's judgment, as I mentioned, gets dislocated; and it's all this other apparatus out there for the bad people. So on the whole I guess I would have to say that the normal and proper and essential meaning of dying with Christ and rising with Christ involves an act of faith, an act of consenting to let go of an identity one has.

Conclusion: normally one would not expect any person to be baptized until he had an old identity which he could consent to let go. To put it another way, baptism is not the sacralization of natural birth; and infant baptism has the effect of making the whole liturgy a sacralization of natural birth and a sacralization of the family. And as Jesus makes clear, the Christian life breaks up the family as a sacred event and breaks up natural childbearing as an [eschatological?] event. But again, when you make infant baptism, that breaking up is obscured, is minimized, is removed, and pretty soon the whole operation of baptism becomes the authorization of having children; natural birth becomes coincident with birth in the life of God, and the family becomes a sacred institution.

VII

Satanic or Christic God

God Does Not Stomp on Satan[1]

The three-fold cause for resistance to death in our time is: 1. Loss, 2. Mutilation, 3. Guilt. The overarching interpretation of death today is extermination understood as the end of all possibilities. 1. Therefore, death is opposed to all affirmative possibilities. All affirmative possibilities are in this present world. Secularity is an ethical mandate. 2. Never relate to death affirmatively. Paul Ramsey is opposed to death with dignity.[2] As anti-human, death can only be seen as dreadful. Therefore, *avoid* death physically and mentally! 3. When death can't be avoided, resist it! Two strategies of resistance: A. Resist death until the last minute. Relax a little—before the

---

1. The title is mine, based, as always, on the text. I had proposed calling this book, *God Does Not Stomp on Satan.* The handwritten manuscript moves in and out of fragmented notes and is found in file folder #107, identified by McGill as "Theol 102—Lectures on Death." These notes seem to be from fall, 1974. The course catalogues of Harvard University Divinity School for the 1970s list many courses taught by McGill (see Appendix: Harvard Divinity School Courses) but no Theology 102 taught by McGill. (A Theology 102 is listed: "Theological Topics and Questions"—Professors Gordon Kaufman and Richard R. Niebuhr [1978–79].) Outline pages with references to "Theol 102," "Lecture I," "Hastings," "Lecture 2," "Lecture 5," "Lecture I" (again) are accompanied by several typed pages of the "Identity and Death" paper (see ch. III), some of which are highly edited with significant handwritten additions. Small outline pages ("Lecture II") are fastened to four unnumbered 8½x11 sheets followed by five numbered sheets ("Lecture 4: Theol 102 on Death Fall 1974"). The remaining pages are headed "Lecture 5" and consist of handwritten sheets with typed "Identity and Death" pages interspersed and edited together with two small sheets—all of this numbered 1–10 with the two final pages of "Identity and Death" at the end. How best to present this material? I have tried to turn McGill's notes into coherent prose without brackets at every turn. When the manuscript settles down a bit, I indicate this. Ch. III—"Identity and Death"—often develops more fully what is only hinted at here.

2. See ch. III, 50.

time of immanent dying. But this is false, for death is the all-embracing possibility. Cf. Martin Heidegger: we experience little deaths.[3] B. Resist more. (Paul Ramsey and Herbert Marcuse.[4]) 1. Death is outside of life as negation of life. 2. One must seek the good in this life. 3. Avoid death in life and thought. 4. Resist death.

Look at death. Death is no *tabula rasa*. Death is already known, understood, and felt in a certain way. No possibility of a simple "Let's understand death" presents itself. We already understand death sufficiently to enter into collision with the New Testament perspective. We today resist death, whereas in the New Testament Christ's death is seen as something to be taken on. We are to join in his dying. How very unintelligible. My lectures have focused on understanding that [in the context of the] three roots of resistance [here McGill turns to the first two pages of "Identity and Death" and loss, mutilation, guilt].

All three components of resistance are actualized in Jesus' death: loss—letting go is not just external—there is no immortal soul; mutilation; and guilt as distinguished from naturalism. But again, the key to resistance today is the image of extermination.

Since you only go around once, go with gusto![5] The good is exclusively in our present situation, our "world." Therefore actualize our world, improve our world. God is not eliminated. God functions in terms of our present situation. God is the cause of the world. God is the idealized perfection of the world. God equals hope. We have our being in and from and toward this world. Therefore we have all our values and good and meaning there as well. God may be transcendent but we are not. Death, as extermination of our being, expresses this positive belief and is always the correlative of this positive belief. [?]

Death ends all possibility of life—a quest, an interpretation, not known. That means that this world is our only possible context for being. Therefore condemnation of those who would find the goodness of life in any other dimension results. Against life after death, against heaven, against negativism. I. [?] preferred life in the world.

Death is antihuman, as total negation of being and value as pertinent to the human. The ethical mandate: II. Avoid death. Don't prettify it, don't naturalize it, don't treat it as one thing among others. Death must always

3. See ch. III, 55–57.

4. See ch. III, 58–62.

5. See ch. III, 54 and n. 19.

be viewed as the dreadful obliteration of value—above all, obliteration to love. Love values another—others: therefore it cannot but be violated by death which obliterates the individual or the community which we love. But if avoidance is in the mandate, that applies to consciousness as well as to action. As the negation of being and value and meaning, death cannot be thought. No one in life should mentally think about it or prepare for it. These are contradictions. Death is not thinkable, as pure nullity. Death can't be prepared for in a positive way. Death is not a value to which the will can be directed. Acceptance may be viewed as necessary but not as intended.

III. Resist. One of the intellectual ventures to oppose death has been the development of medicine. Medicine works to prevent death from occurring as long as possible.[6] People become physicians because they want to resist death.

A strange tension is to be found in medical work, which uses the study of nature to resist death. But death is natural, is inherent in nature. Not only life [?], but animal life is nourished by life dying. Eating maintains metabolism by death. The organism has its living system taken into another.

Yet in their motives physicians do not look upon death as natural and acceptable. The death of a patient is taken by them as somehow their own personal failure. They work to resist death, delay death, prevent death. The study of nature provides them with a means and not with a philosophy, a value perspective. Now that physicians have succeeded in delaying death, their total unconnection [sic.] with the natural has become clear. It is hard for them to let people die naturally, hard for them—psychically, morally hard and not just legally hard for them to stop their prolonging life by extraordinary means. Given certain degrees of suffering or certain degrees of drugged coma, is life worth maintaining? Even as extermination, isn't death preferable to some conditions of life? Nature gives death against excessive suffering and coma.

A major intellectual effort to oppose death has been the study of history. Like medicine, it is an effort to oppose the negating power of death, not before death comes, but after death has come.

Death is inevitable. To resist is fine, but doomed. Warning about societal ways of resisting death—ways as efforts to challenge, master and instrumentalize death—is in order. Therefore, if we could accept death,

6. McGill here refers to "Feifel's studies" without specific reference. See Herman Feifel, ed., *The Meaning of Death* (New York: McGraw-Hill, 1959). Herman Feifel, born in 1915, is an American psychologist contributing significantly to the development of the field of thanatology.

motivation for this [resisting] would be loss. An admonition to physicians: unless you can accept death, your relations to your patients will be pathological. You will have to abandon them when you can no longer cure them. Consider Avery Weisman—care stops with cure.[7] Seek how to approach death by studying the dying. Five stages: Denial = in life, Anger, Bargaining, Depression, Acceptance.[8] Therefore, from the dying, physicians and society can learn to accept death; concretely that means staying with dying persons, in their process of dying; that means physicians may learn not to fear them, to avoid them, to look upon them as their failures.[9]

Contemporary experience rejects this framework. Death is not at the end of natural life. The old view is chronological: there is the time of life, then death, then after death. This view has gone, vanished.

Two challenges to the reassuring view appear.

A. Confrontation with nothingness may be in life, not just at the end in death—usually in isolation, meaninglessness, and no identity. "Death" loses its objective, empirical focus. The same is met earlier in loss of identity: I am nameless. <u>Kenneth Fearing</u>.[10] We do not cope by chronological distinctions. Mass society has cheapened life. Secularism believes that being in the world is real, is life, is positive: death is nullifying. Not at all. The world is nullifying.

The same is true of death, not as nullity, but as mutilation. Mutilation is in life, not just at the end. Look at oppression. People have their whole

---

7. Is McGill moving from a "negative" withdrawal of care to a "positive" withdrawal of care—abandonment of care when cure seems not possible and abandonment of care when cure is accomplished? McGill gives no references, but Weisman seems to write of negative withdrawal: ". . . physicians have continued to believe that their responsibility ends when a patient passes into that limbo of life, called the terminal phase. Nothing more can be done, it is solemnly said, usually in a pious whisper, and the treatment ends. But *when* the terminal phase beings is left ambiguous" (Avery D. Weisman, MD, *The Realization of Death: A Guide for the Psychological Autopsy* [New York: Jason Aronson, Inc., 1974], 25). But Weisman also writes, "If cure is impossible, then care and safe conduct ensure a dignified exitus. It is our mutual obligation" (190). See also Weisman, *On Dying and Denying: A Psychiatric Study of Terminality* (New York: Behavioral Publications, Inc., 1972), 223, 225. Avery Weisman, born in 1913, is Professor of Psychiatry Emeritus, Harvard Medical School, Harvard University.

8. McGill is here following Elisabeth Kübler-Ross, *On Death and Dying*. See ch. III, 53 and n. 18.

9. To this sentence from "Identity and Death" (see ch. III, 53)—"This educational effort is motivated in part by a compassion for the dying and of a desire to 'make their last days more tranquil'"—McGill has written in: "How? By sitting listening."

10. See below, 128–29 and n. 13.

lives' continuity deformed, twisted, tormented. Death as terminal event may be the extreme of mutilation, mutilation reaching to and strangling the taproot of life and identity. But mutilations are in life. So it is impossible to contrast life and death on chronological grounds. Death is on-going experience. What happens in death happens also in life. The structure of life can become so negating of meaning and identity, so oppressive and mutilating that persons lose a sense of life. This is not just using death metaphorically. The anti-human is also in life, an anti-human that reaches toward the roots of meaning and life. Secularity's roots are [in?] the world: but what if the world is killing?

But still one human act is possible, as William Wantling's poem, "Just Lately,"[11] [reminds us]. Become inhuman. Don't fight it, be [lacerated?] by it. How [?]?

B. The other challenge: life-structures yield death, work for death. Death is not end of the life-region. Energies of and processes of life work to deliver death, are implicated in death. Nuclear war. Pollution. Overpopulation. And not only in these ways do life-processes deliver death. But because of the terrible results of death, life works against it everywhere. Life is not what happens before death comes; life is a resistance. The physician embodies a feature of everyone's existence. Love, [especially?] sexual love, can be a dissolution of the self [to be?] death against death.[12]

The meaning of ego and self has changed. There is no viable sense of "soul." All these changes have changed the question of death and the possibility of life after death. We do not overcome death chronologically by a time after death. Rather the notion is of transcendence or of meaning

11. See below, 132–33 and n. 21.

12. Here McGill references (without quoting) James Dickey, *Eye-Beaters*, 14. This page number does not correspond with the page numbers in the edition I have located. The poem is six pages long—and challenging. Perhaps McGill is referring to lines such as these (the spacing is Dickey's): "They are blind. Listen listen well / To your walking that gathers the blind in bonds gather these / Who have fought with themselves have blacked their eyes wide / Open, toddling like dolls and like penguins soft-knotted down, / Protected, arms bound to their sides in gauze, but dark is not / To be stood in that way: they holler howl till they can shred / Their gentle ropes whirl and come loose. They *know* they should see / But *what*, now? When their fists smash their eyeballs, they behold no / Stranger giving light from his palms. What they glimpse has flared / In mankind from the beginning. In the asylum, children turn to go back / Into the race . . ." See James Dickey, *The Eye-Beaters, Blood, Victory, Madness, Buckhead and Mercy* (Garden City, New York: Doubleday and Company, Inc., 1970), 50–55; quoted lines are from 50. James Dickey (1923–1997) was a American poet. He was appointed Poet Laureate Consultant in Poetry to the Library of Congress in 1966.

in this life. One important change: confrontation with nothingness is not focused upon the moment of death. There is a strong sense of nothingness in life—vacuity, meaninglessness, radical alienation. Kenneth Fearing's "American Rhapsody (4)" [captures this]:

> First you bite your fingernails. And then you comb your hair
>   Again. And then you wait. And wait.
> (They say, you know, that first you lie. And then you steal, they
>   say. And then, they say, you kill.)
>
> Then the doorbell rings. Then Peg drops in. And Bill. And Jane.
>   And Doc.
> And first you talk, and smoke, and hear the news and have a
>   Drink. Then you walk down the stairs.
> And you dine, then, and go to a show after that, perhaps, and
>   after that a night spot, and after that come home again,
>   and climb the stairs again, and again go to bed.
>
> But first Peg argues, and Doc replies. First you dance the same
>   dance and you drink the same drink you always drank
>   before.
> And the piano builds a roof of notes above the world.
> And the trumpet weaves a dome of music through space. And the
>   drum makes a ceiling over space and time and night.
> And then the table-wit. And then the check. Then home again
>   to bed.
> But first, the stairs.
>
> And do you now, baby, as you climb the stairs, do you still feel
>   as you felt back there?
> Do you feel again as you felt this morning? And the night be-
>   fore? And then the night before that?
>
> (They say, you know, that first you hear voices. And then you
>   have visions, they say. Then, they say, you kick and
>   scream and rave.)
>
> Or do you feel: What is one more night in a lifetime of nights?
> What is one more death, or friendship, or divorce out of two,
>   or three? Or four? Or five?
> One more face among so many, many faces, one more life among
>   so many million lives?

But first, baby, as you climb and count the stairs (and they total
    the same) did you, sometime or somewhere, have a dif-
    ferent idea?
Is this, baby, what you were born to feel, and do, and be?[13]

The nothingness also encountered in death is [now?] in life. Death is identified with loss of identity—I am nameless—and with loss of meaning (Kenneth Fearing).

The key: we do not [cope?] by dualism—this life versus the next life,
the natural versus the *temporal*, spiritual, temporal versus the eternal. [This
is very important. Here Christian faith is in no need of challenging culture.
This level of awareness is the matrix which the gospel forms or transforms
rather than discredits.][14] [?]: therefore secularists who explore nihilism and
meaning are relevant for theology, especially since dogmatic answers seem
unrelated.

a) Today the experience of death is made up of so many layers.

b) Today death penetrates all layers of life: technological war, geno-
cide, mass famine. Politics may risk the survival of the race. Love works
against death yet is like death. There are no natural structures limiting,
locating death [or love]. An Old Testament prophet proclaims: death has
come up into our chambers.[15]

This is opposed to a medical, biological view of death where death is
about the end of life. This is opposed to Kübler-Ross and the concern to
consult the dying regarding death.

13. "American Rhapsody (4)," Kenneth Fearing, *Collected Poems of Kenneth Fearing*
(New York: Random House, 1940), 131–132. McGill does not quote this poem but references it, and the reason for its reference is manifest. Three "American Rhapsody" poems
do precede (4). The first two are in a section of *Collected Poems* called simply "Poems
(1930–1935)." A brief indication of content is impossible and would betray the poetry.
"Maimed in the expiation of living" is some indication of (1), 44. "As though" hints at but
far from exhausts "American Rhapsody (2)": "as though there were love . . . as though
there could be laughter . . ." (64). "American Rhapsody (3)" is in a section of *Collected
Poems* titled "Dead Reckoning (1935–1938)." McGill might well have referenced—and
quoted—this poem: "Tomorrow, yes, tomorrow . . . bona-fide life will arrive at last . . ."
(Wanna bet?) Bitterist irony shines out of the "silver" theme: "Rockets, rockets, Roman
candles, flares, will burst in every corner / of the night, to veil with snakes of silvery fire
the noth- / ingness that waits and waits . . . Tomorrow, yes tomorrow, surely we begin
at last to live . . ." (92). (Wanna bet?) "American Rhapsody (4)" is in "The Agency (New
Poems) (1938–1940)" section of *Collected Poems*. Kenneth Fearing (1902–1961) was an
American poet, novelist, and journalist.

14. The brackets are McGill's.

15. No reference is given. Was McGill thinking of Isaiah 26:20–21?

Kübler-Ross' mentality locates death in the hospital. This medical view belongs to the old chronological dualism: natural life versus death with death at end. Kübler-Ross tries to construe people's attitude on this basis: a)—time of imminent dying, b)—watch changing attitudes; no rational component; stages like impersonal attitudes are not connected with other experiences, c)—death is an external necessity. [No?] [interpretations?] possible or relevant d)—no one their own death: Rilke [on] sickness and disease in medicine.[16]

For people: individual death is minor, is a hint of large deaths—war, famine, nuclear.

Thanatolatry: death is absolute for being: extermination. In power, death is supreme; in value, life or world or God are supreme. Paul Ramsey argues for opposition to death, acknowledging its total negativity. Even Heidegger makes death absolute on the positive side. We live inauthentically, beyond ourselves as extensions of the world, of society, of others. Death as a property of our being—not as an external event—proves that there is no hope to secure ourselves by being extensions of the world and shows that our reality is not of that sort. Death redeems us to be ourselves, to become authentic.

I will examine three elements, three emphases that are ingredient in Jesus' suffering and dying.[17]

I. Crucifixion represents one of the most tortuous forms of execution that has been discovered. Extreme pain is combined with public humiliation, since the body's behavior in pain and as death approaches becomes a source of fascination and ribald humor. The Latin word for torture was *cruciare*, to crucify. Consider our word "excruciation." The process of execution by crucifixion is only the climax in the passion narratives to traditions about trials and traditions about Jesus' rejection by his own followers—Judas' betrayal, Peter's denial, the flight of all rest [see Matt 26:14–16, 56, 69–75, Mark 14:10–11, 50, 66–72, Luke 22:3–6, 56–62].

A. If Jesus is the Messiah, God's own representative, the bearer and actualization of God's will and presence—then this response on the part of people is staggering. One move is to see something peculiar about these people. They are odd or queerly perverse. Against this is the consideration that the impact of Jesus in every generation and condition of

16. Rainer Maria Rilke (1875–1926) was born in Prague and became one of the greatest of modern poets. McGill gives a reference—"See [a two-word title (underlined)]"—which I am unable to decipher.

17. From this point, the manuscript becomes more coherent.

people provokes resistance. Perhaps fear awakens the will to destroy him in our feeling that he threatens our most basic values. He therefore must be eliminated and thus discredited in his claims regarding God—since anyone whom we can kill is obviously not the bearer of God's power and authority. But if there is not a positive will to destroy him, at least a preference to desert him in his dying [is manifest]. Follow the disciples. His dying discredits him, makes him dangerous to us. The study of the negative reaction is the study of sin. The power of Jesus sets people's teeth on edge—has set, is setting and will set people in violent opposition. Most sobering: those priests and procurators are not the refuse of human society. They are the upholders and actualizers of human values.

B. Jesus' response is not revenge, not reciprocal obliteration. Even as resurrected, Jesus' response to his death is not to destroy those enemies.[18] As bearer and the presence of God's will and glory and power, Jesus does not disclose God's aggressions against those who mock him and mutilate his representative, his Messiah. There is not only no hint of this. There are traditions which exclude this. For example, "Father, forgive them, for they know not what they do" [Luke 23:34]. So far as Jesus is perceived to be God with us, God Emmanuel, then his response to his ordeal is a living out of the prohibition against revenge: turn the other cheek [see Matt 5:39, Luke 6:29], etc. This ethic is primarily the ethic of God's dealing with people as exhibited in relation to the crucifixion. Only secondarily, is this an ethics for people.

Now this is basic in an understanding of God. Precisely the directness of the attack on God means that revenge is not God's way. The less God is involved in Jesus, the less Jesus' failure to be aggressive and retributive has to do with God.[19] But if Jesus is God's own reality, in some unique and special way, and if such brutal degradation does not elicit revenge from God, then this means something fundamental about the character of God. It means human aggressions and blasphemies and opposition do not force God into the same mode. It means that God and humanity do not meet on the same terms, answering each other in the same way. If humanity receives

18. See Williams, *Resurrection*, ch. IV, 77, n. 3 and ch. V, 98, n. 21.

19. Initially, this is puzzling. We might expect: "The more God is involved in Jesus, the more Jesus' failure to be aggressive and retributive has to do with God." This is precisely what McGill goes on to say. So the "less" language means: but this is not the case. Or if we do not see the character of God as manifested in Jesus, we do not see Jesus' "failure to be aggressive and retributive" as revelatory of God.

God's love with violent destruction, God does not answer with violent destruction.

But this is unnerving and dizzying. Without punishment, how can human behavior be controlled, be conditioned? [Think of the] bishops at Vatican II: We need a doctrine of hell to keep people in moral behavior. If human aggression is not met with counter aggression, what will inhibit it? Obviously the point is not to inhibit aggression but to remove it, not to control behavior but purify the heart [see James 4:8]. "You have heard it said, 'Do not commit murder or you will be brought to judgment.' But I tell you this: Anyone who nurses anger against his neighbor must be brought to judgment" (Matt 5:21 [NEB—roughly]). Not outer behavior but inner motive is the focus. Then the importance of God's retribution changed. Paul saw Jesus as a new dispensation by God over against the dispensation to the Jews. How new? Fulfilling the law was no longer a condition for a right relation to God. In all this, Paul is responding to Jesus' failure to revenge the crucifixion.[20]

C. I have been speaking of how Jesus' non-revenge for the cross alters the understanding of God. But this also alters our understanding of suffering and death. In some sense, they are not as devastating as was believed. If death is absolute, in [sic.] radical, if its [sic.] cuts to root of being and value, if it undoes all that being can attain—such is the myth of extermination—then anyone with a knife or a gun can impose that on other persons.

I spoke of the three-fold ethic associated with extermination: to seek the good in this life, to avoid death and thought of [wish?] for death, to resist death. But there is a fourth ethic, never proclaimed but impossible to avoid. If death is so absolute at the level of power, anyone can deliver that power upon others. However null in terms of value, in this view death is seen as absolute in terms of power. Where the value being threatened is a people's or an individual's power—and not their goodness—why not perform death? [Here McGill notes] Wantling's poem.

> just lately
> I've seen through it
> I've seen through it all
> once, you know I was quite religious
> but now
> there is nothing
> nothing

20. Again, see Williams, *Resurrection*, ch. IV, 77, n. 3 and ch. V, 98, n. 21.

yet still I pray

O Nothing, that
which is Naught
    please
do not kill me with your
drab despicable days of
loss, of dumb terror
fulfilled, of pain . . .

You! you . . . <u>peasants</u>
you wouldn't know just
how much I need to laugh
    my god
how badly I only
      <u>want</u> <u>to</u> <u>laugh</u>

& what if the dam should
    suddenly burst
if suddenly I should run
headlong, frothing, haphazardly
hurling shrapnel grenades
into high-noon crowds?
if suddenly tossing aside the
    dead ugly ache of it
all, I equaled the senseless
with my brute senseless act?

O My, wouldn't I
Shine? wouldn't
I shine then?
wouldn't it be <u>I</u> then who
had created God
at last?[21]

21. William Wantling, *The Source* (El Cerrito, CA: Dust Book, 1966), 19. The poem is untitled in the book but is listed in the Contents as "Just Lately." There is a tiny, faint line in the manuscript under "Wantling's poem." I can make out only part of it: "Two [motives?] for hate: defend good versus attack [??] avoid impotence." William Wantling (1933–1974) was an American poet and Professor of English at Illinois State University, 1970–1974.

The myth of extermination, of real negation by death, invites killing. So those who kill Jesus. "Death" for them is redeeming. It destroys and eliminates evil. It preserves their values against a profound threat. Those who desert Jesus acknowledge this power of death. [Yet] the absence of revenge [suggests] that death and suffering are not that serious. Fundamental values are not lost. In failing to revenge, God is not allowing enormous evil. Jesus' execution and murder are carried [through?]. [There is] no stopping [this] and no later revenge. Relative to something else, death and blasphemy and the will to destroy [to do?] possess finality.[22] Death is desacralized. God does not impose it to vindicate the holy. Death is only one strand in a complex negation. Evil is desacralized. God is beyond good and evil.

I will focus on a specific pattern developed by the Gospel of John. The Gospel of John presents Jesus under two aspects: the Incarnation where the logos becomes flesh, and the passion. The first aspect constitutes the meaning of Jesus' ministry—his teachings and especially his signs, his miracles. The extraordinary thing about Jesus, in John's portrayal, is the fact that he exists in a relationship of reciprocal "in-being" with God. He exists as incorporated into union with the Father—not a physical union where all identities are dissolved—but a participatory union. Jesus shares in God's will and knowledge and power and life. He does so by virtue of God's giving him this union. In other words, for John, this union of Jesus with the Father is a loving gift by the Father. And Jesus receives his existence in this union and lives it as a gift of love. His whole self-understanding is constituted on gratitude. John uses the noun "glory" ([δόξα], doxa) to designate this existence of Jesus in union with God: "The logos became flesh. He came to dwell among us and we saw his glory, such glory as befits God's only son, full of grace and truth" (John 1:14, NEB—nearly). Glory here is identical with the union of love—with God's giving and Jesus' gratitude. God's giving and Jesus' gratitude mark the innermost center of Jesus' being. He receives from God, not just conditions for his existence, not just powers for his existence. His central being is located at its roots in union with God, is nourished and established in God's order of reality. He comes from the Father, not once upon a time, mythically. His being is constantly established as coming from God. And because he receives union with God at his center, because he constantly receives himself from God as within God's life and

---

22. McGill writes, "Relative to something else, death ~~does not~~ . . ." "Does not" is scratched out, yet the point would seem to be that death does *not* possess finality; though "relative to something else," it may.

power, therefore gratitude is his most fundamental attitude at the core of his consciousness. In every act of his being, he knows that this *is* an act of a being he receives in union with God his origin. Gratitude belongs inherently to him. John's concise statement of this glory: the Father is in me and I am in the Father.[23] This glory is observed by the disciples. This glory is disclosed in Jesus' miracles, especially in the rising of Lazarus [see John 11:1–44]. Such is the first aspect of John's Gospel.

The second aspect focuses on Jesus' passion—his mutilation and death. And here John also uses the term glory, but not the noun. In connection with Jesus' death, John uses the verb, "to be glorified" [δοξασθῇ, *doxasthē*]. "The hour has come for the Son of Man to be glorifed. In truth I tell you, a grain of wheat remains a solitary grain unless it falls into the ground and dies; but if it dies, it bears a rich harvest" (John 12:23, NEB). The hour has come—the hour of his death—for the Son of Man to be glorified. Now—when Judas had gone out to lead the priests to seize Jesus [see John 13:30–31]—"Now the Son of Man is glorified, and in him God is glorified" (John 13:31, NEB). Again in Jesus' prayer: "Father the hour has come. Glorify your Son, that the Son may glorify you" (John 17:1, NEB).

Now notice carefully: apparently there is a glory which Jesus has lacked, notwithstanding his union with God. This glory he receives at his death. But this is also a glory which God has lacked and which is supplied to God by Jesus' death. What is this glory? Jesus is already in God, already lives in union with God's life. What can this extra glory be? [Let us consider again the] passage in John 12:23: When a grain of wheat falls and dies, it bears a rich harvest. That is, by his death, the glory which he shares with the Father expands to include his followers. He extends his glory—his life in loving union with God—to the human race. He extends the life that was in him to others. By his death, he bears a rich harvest. For John, the glory which Jesus bestows on his followers consists in their being in Jesus and Jesus in them. This is the glory he wins by his death. Through his death, he comes to be in his followers, and his followers come to be in him. He extends to them the relationship between himself and God. But that loving union is primarily and essentially God's doing. Therefore, the Son has and does nothing of his own. If Jesus is glorified by gathering his followers into himself, into his life, that "himself" and that "his life" is actually the doing

---

23. "Do you not believe that I am in the Father, and the Father in me? I am not myself the source of the words I speak to you: it is the Father who dwells in me doing his own work. Believe me when I say that I am in the Father and the Father in me . . ." (John 14:10–11, NEB).

of God, so that this also enhances the glory of God, the active union of love which God establishes. Jesus is glorifed on the cross in that he gathers people into the reciprocal relationship of in-being which subsists between himself and God. "The glory which you have given me I have given them, that they may be one as we are one" (17:22, NEB). What is this glory? It is the gift made by Jesus to his followers by which they are found together in union with one another and become sharers in Jesus' union with the Father. Glory is identical with love. "Greater love has no one than to lay down one's life for one's friends" [John 15:13].

Now we can see here a radical re-understanding of death. First of all, death is the complete undoing, the complete loss of possessed reality. From the perspective of the technique of having,[24] it is the final extermination, because death means a person is dispossessed of all reality. A person possesses in himself or herself no immortal soul, no everlasting spirit, no indestructible life-principle. In death, a person's entire possessed being passes away from him or her and into the world. In himself or herself, he or she is nothing at all. But notice carefully. He or she is nothing at all, *in himself or in herself*. But is that the end?

Not at all. For in truth, if we are to understand our existence in terms of Jesus, we do not exist by virtue of that reality which has been delivered over into our possession. In and through and as Jesus,[25] we exist by the giving of God.

On Wednesday, I developed what I see as the perspective of the gospel of John—in particular, John's emphasis on the death of Jesus as the process by which the life which Jesus shares with God is communicated to others. Note: John uses the analogy of nature. In nature, death is nourishment. Life is nourished by ingestion: death is [often?] communication. Eating and drinking. This is only an *analogy* of what is encountered in Jesus—but a real analogy. Power in Jesus is the ground of this nature. There are two sides: 1) this is through the form of human existence; 2) such is the case because this is the power of God in which human existence shares.

Look at anthropology and theology. Look at anthropology first. Where death is a communication of life, it lies within life. It is essential

24. This phrase and theme are found throughout McGill's papers. See ch. VI, 107, n. 2.

25. This is vital—literally. McGill's meaning must be not that we exist *as Jesus* but that we exist as Jesus *existed*—and *exists*.

for life—not for life as possessed but for life as shared. Be fruitful means to expend one's own life.

[Now McGill notes: "Hastings, p. 36." Two closely edited pages from "Identity and Death" follow.[26]] This means that death as expenditure and communication is a vital act. Jesus' crucifixion is the extension of his vitality to us, the coming into full life of his aliveness. Therefore the day of that event can only be an extraordinarily good Friday. This also means that, since Jesus' death is essentially and literally an event of our nourishment, it can only be re-presented by eating and drinking.

But this seems like a paradox or contradiction. How can anyone lay down *his own* life, the life which he himself is? What else can this be but an act of self-extermination?

Such would indeed be the case so far as persons had their being and identity in terms of their own reality, i.e., in terms of those selves and that vital energy which lie at their own disposal. But such is not the human condition in Jesus. Through Jesus our identity lies not within ourselves but in the constant receiving of ourselves from God. This means that we *are* not our present lives; we who are this receiving from God only "have" our present lives. Our being is not identical with our having; it is identical to our receiving. We are not the same as our actual lives. As those who focus their being in the constituting activity of God, persons are free to let go of their lives for others, not as if their lives were their true and only identity, their essential selves, but as if their lives were something at their disposal, something which they could really and freely use for themselves or for others, something to which they stand in a relation of freedom. In being from God and in God, they are also free to give all that they have already received to others. They may do this: there is no compulsive necessity. The whole ethical life thus shifts its center of gravity. My reality is not dependent on how well I can nourish, sustain, and perfect that being that I already possess within myself. It is dependent on God's constituting, and because God's constituting is not blocked by princes, powers, or life or death [see Rom 8:38–39], I am free to communicate my possessed being ecstatically to others. "It is by this that we know what love is: that Christ laid down his life for us. And we in turn are bound to lay down our lives for our brothers" (1 John 3:16, NEB). If we see another in need, when we have enough for

26. See ch. III, 70–71.

ourselves,[27] and close our hearts to that person, then we are not living by the truth. In fact, we are not living at all; we are sterile and dead.

But if this is so, note how this affects our aim to help our neighbor. Why feed the hungry and clothe the naked and shelter the homeless? Why heal the sick and visit the imprisoned? The answer is clear: not to give them bits of reality for them to hold onto, so that by the possession of something they can secure their identity. Others are nourished with the freedom to *give themselves away.*[28]

Let me now turn to the theological element. The activity of Jesus is as such the activity of God. Jesus is by receiving from God and sharing in God and being himself on the basis of God. Jesus' human way is what it is because it is the perfect participation in and actualization of God's own proper way. God does not die—against Altizer:[29] a sense of God as inexhaustible. For God to communicate does never empty God of the being which God has. A creature receives and lets go. This is not inexhaustible. But in receiving and letting go, a creature repeats in its terms the character which marks God at God's level. That is, giving and receiving are constitutive of ultimate reality, of foundational reality. Therefore, God is constituted of these activities and therefore of agents of these activities. The old language of Father and Son, generator and generated, is electrical. "Originator" is too external. [What of the] French *parent* ["*n. m.* (*fem.* parente) Relative, kinsman, kinswoman; (*pl.*) parents, father and mother, relatives, kindred"[30]]? Off-spring. [What of] other names? "Father" is the name for agent that gives. "Son" is the name for agent that receives, receives radically, that possesses nothing out of itself, that receives all its being constantly from the originator. Heir. Issue. Chip of [off] the old block.[31] Off-spring. It is important to use variety as opposed to [solidifying?] as Father and Son. The receiver is fully God:

27. This phrase puzzles me and seems so unMcGillian, given McGill's diatribe against philanthrophy. See, e.g., *Sermons of Arthur C. McGill*, 8–9, 120.

28. A note in McGill's outline for these lectures (see 123, n. 1) can now serve as a kind of summary of this discussion: "How can Jesus lay down his life? He is not what he possesses. Help others to be givers: come to them in need."

29. See Thomas J. J. Altizer, *The Gospel of Christian Atheism* (Philadelphia: Westminster, 1966), e.g., 71: "The radical Christian knows that God has truly died in Jesus and that his death has liberated humanity from the oppressive presence of the primordial Being." See McGill, "The Death of God and All That," 45–58, esp. 54–55.

30. *Cassell's French-English English-French Dictionary*, ed. Ernest A. Baker, new ed. revised J. L. Manchon (New York: Funk & Wagnalls Company, 1951), 519.

31. I add "Like father, like son"—but "like" is no vote for "*homoiousias*" over "*homoousias*": just the opposite.

is the duplication of God's reality and still is essentially receiving. These are not two autonomous Gods—but really two. The key is that neediness is constitutive of God. Neediness is not the mark of the creature as over against God.

God's being involves radical, total dependence. God is not constituted by having, but by giving and receiving. That is to read God's character from Jesus.[32] The poor belong to Jesus, are one with Jesus. Jesus has nothing of his own. The immediate result of this theology—this characterization of God is that it stands opposed to another notion of God where being is understood as possession and power is understood as domination. Being as possession means that God is seen as absolute with our notion of absoluteness. What is this notion? Our hated of our creatureliness. This God is a construct of our own self-hatred. Over against this is the conception of being as giving and receiving, as always and inherently communal and dynamic. When power is construed as domination, the lordship of the absolute is usually imaged as his power to get his own way. This is not the power to make the other fruitful. This is the power to make others subject to it. An important clarification here is that the originator constitutes, shares, and freely withdraws. Its constituting is not simply an extension of itself. Its constituting involves an [othering?] coordinated with [dependence?] and sharing.

Images are inadequate and collide. The temptation is to worship dominative power. The point of contrast is the relation to need: threatening need as contrasted with nourishing need. [In relation to threatening need], dominative power is final. In the New Testament, Satanic power is the power of domination: Bow down and worship me and I will give you all kingdoms of world [see Matt 4:8–10, Luke 4:5–8]. There is no bowing down to the divinity of Jesus Christ. Canon 20 of Nicaea prohibits kneeling at Mass.[33] We are constituted by God of God's own aliveness. There is no abasement. Only Satanic power is honored by self-abasement.

---

32. Italics added. In these pages, I have become careless with brackets—neglecting them—in quest of coherent prose.

33. "The Canons of the 318 Holy Fathers Assembled in the City of Nice, in Bithynia" (A.D. 325): "Canon XX. Forasmuch as there are certain persons who kneel on the Lord's Day and in the days of Pentecost, therefore, to the intent that all things may be uniformly observed everywhere (in every parish), it seems good to the holy Synod that prayer be made to God standing." See *The Seven Ecumenical Councils of the Undivided Church: Their Canons and Dogmatic Decrees*, ed. Henry R. Percival, ed. (Oxford: James Parker and Company, 1900), A Select Library of Nicene and Post-Nicene Fathers of the Christian Church, Second Series, vol. XIV, 8, 42.

Through Jesus Christ, what claims to be power is not final power, essential power, decisive power. The cross which seemed like the killing of God's own turned out to be the most profound communication of life.

Now look at Karl Barth.[34] I have two points of difficulty with Barth.

A. Human sin is to judge good and evil[35]—to judge good and evil on our terms, with our competence [CD, IV/I, 231–233]. Sin [is] to be like God in this regard. Barth's understanding of the opposite is obedience. But obedience in a special sense: letting God direct us regarding good and evil, being dependent on God in this. The content of obedience is acknowledging God as *supreme* and ourselves as subject [CD, IV/I, 232–234].

My view is that it is the calling of human existence to be like God, to be godly. Be perfect as your Father in heaven is perfect [see Matt 5:48]. As God has loved us, so let us love one another [see 1 John 4:7–21]. Sin, therefore, is not: I want to be like God. Sin is to have a wrong sense of God, whether that involves worship or resentment. Sin begins in the belief that God's divinity consists in God dominating me and requiring my abasement [see CD, IV/I, 233]. This precipitates a reaction of rejection and the desire to be like *this* God. Barth seems trapped in this circle. God is superior, authoritative—the big boss. Obedience is acknowledging God's supremacy. The alternative to sin is really to receive, to be in one's receiving. To obey God is to have a will conformed to the actuality of God, to God's own character. God as originator means that God moves to the other to constitute and to give value to the other. My obedience is not my abasement to God's superiority but my willing both receiving and the aim of God. God's being constitutes good. My obedience is to value that good, to enjoy it and extend it and nourish it.

God is not Satanic—not asserting himself by subordinating everything else. The receiving in God is not second, subordinate, because the originator holds nothing back and shares all. Barth suggests that there is a first and a second in God. No. There is a giving and a receiving, and therefore a structural first and second, but not a value first and second. The second is totally equal to the first and cannot in any way belittle itself with reference to the first. If the second belittled itself with reference to first, then it would deny that the first shared all and would testify to a Satanic God and not a Christic God.

34. Barth's work received central treatment in McGill's doctoral dissertation, *The Place of Dogmatic Theology in the University*, Yale University, 1961.

35. See Karl Barth, *Church Dogmatics*, eds. G. W. Bromiley and T. F. Torrance, trans. G. W. Bromiley (Edinburgh: T. & T. Clark, 1956), The Doctrine of Reconciliation, IV, I, 231. (Hereafter in text: CD, IV/I.)

B. For Barth the cross is the abolition of sin. God negates, destroys, and annihilates sin in the death of Jesus. Death is negation, destruction, and annihilation. God contradicts the world that contradicts God. I have a theological problem with this characteristic of God. That problem is Satanic power. In the face of need, this Satanic power establishes itself by the power to destroy. Destruction is its mark. Jesus says to the Pharisees: "You are children of your Father the Devil, who was a murderer from the beginning" [see John 8:44]. The Satanic exercises killing as its unique and decisive exercise of power. All victimization and oppression by people of one another depends on the power to kill. For Barth, this is God's power *vis-à-vis* sin. God does to sin what sin does. In dealing with sin, God takes on the character of the Satanic. He annihilates, he murders. Though it is his own [son] that bears sin and is subject to murder.

1. But what of the triumph of evil? Does "death" also abolish? This seems to imply that sin has a being that has to be undone, i.e., made into non-being. Only by non-being is sin handled. Yes, Jesus' cross is also [?] of evil. Evil equals a pattern of power. Negation of power is key.

2. Satanic power's essential character is to destroy—"murderer from the beginning."

3. I am not sure God also establishes his power as but Satanic in opposition to Satan's destructiveness. My reticence: God does not stomp on Satan, does not outdominate domination, does not prove his superiority to Satan in Satanic terms. Why not? As the cross shows, the intention to destroy is not stopped. It does not have to be.

The intention to destroy *doesn't* have enough power. It can't reach beyond the one being killed. It can't stop this one's extending its aliveness. It can't deny this one the freedom to give his life to others. The key: God is not God because the Satanic is destroyed Satanically. God is God even where the Satanic is operating because the Satanic is impotent, is not God. Barth's notion of the cross as annihilation of sin imputes to God both destruction and love, both Satanic violence and Christic love. I believe in God the nourisher almighty.[36]

---

36. I have reversed the last two sentences.

VIII

Theological Fragments[1]

By bringing together a variety of Christians who are convinced and articulate, everyone is better able to realize how unmanageably diverse and universal is the gospel of Jesus.

I no more limit creativity to scholarship and art than I limit Christ to Sunday.

The connection between God and the human in terms of creativity is not easy to hold in focus.

. . . [P]atience, persistence and holding out against discouragement or social rejection are all crucial for creativity. Creativity is not some elixir in and of itself. It is an excess that, when it occurs, puts an extra strain on all the other human strengths. By itself creativity never accomplished anything.[2]

Oh would that there was truth in the intercourse between persons! One person defends Christianity and another attacks it. In the end, if one examines their lives, neither of them bothers very much about it. Perhaps it is (only) their livelihood.[3]

---

1. I am playing off of Johannes Climacus' (Søren Kierkegaard's) *Philosophiske Smuler* (*Philosophical Fragments*).

2. From "Congress of Laity, Evaluation by Arthur C. McGill" (file #237): North American Congress of the Laity, 17–20 February, 1978, Hyatt Regency Hotel, Los Angeles. McGill attended as a member of the "Critique Committee."

3. No quotation marks and no reference accompany these words in a slim folder (#23) headed in McGill's hand: "Good Quotes for Theology." The entry is preceded by "Kierk"—McGill's abbreviation for Kierkegaard. If this is not a quotation from Kierkegaard, it well might be.

In a letter to "Dear John,"[4] McGill writes:

The point I would have to reject is your identification of Christian love with fellowship and *personal intimacy*, and your confident assumption that Christ's command to us to love was based on the fact that love would remove the agonies in social relations by giving them a personal intimacy.

This notion that the meaning love is to bring intimacy into human relations and is to remove all feeling of strangeness and uneasiness from our attitudes toward each other has prevented Christians from saying anything very relevant to human problems.

1. Being strange to each other is part of the meaning of being a person. Not to feel the uneasiness of strangeness when in the presence of another is only possible by forgetting that the other is a free person, whose behavior you cannot predict and whose mystery you can never remove. A love which seeks the pleasure and security of intimacy is a love which wants to take the other for granted, to reduce the relation to one of pure comfort and pleasure, with none of the awe and uneasiness that we feel with a stranger.

2. By identifying Christian love with friendliness and intimacy, the prevailing view which you share has made Christ's command of love preposterously irrelevant for man. If men are strangers to each other and will remain so as long as they are genuinely human, if no amount of common life, shared experience, or mutual understanding can remove their freedom to be different and unexpected, then the proper ethic is not one which encourages people to try to remove this sense of strangeness, but one which teaches them to live *with it*.

   a. What does an ethic of intimacy and mutual understanding have to say to men in the modern city, where the neighbor and the employer and the policeman and the whole mass of people who keep flowing against us remain strangers? All it seems to say is that at that level of relationship no real morality is possible, and so leaves most city life in an amoral wilderness.

   b. What does such an ethic say to nations which must face each other through different languages, different cultures, different histories, and different values? It can only say: the sole basis of fruitful relations is mutual understanding, mutual intimacy—which is to say, the removal of our strangeness. And what does

4.. "Princeton University, Princeton, N. J., November 13, 1961"—from folder #361.

this mean in practice? It means that we try to Americanize other countries, giving them industrial know-how and democratic governments. Why? Not for their sake, but to remove their strangeness so that we can satisfy our frustrated effort to "love" them.

c. What does such an ethic have to say to couples who have been married a year or so, are beginning to discover the recesses of strangeness in each other behind the surface of shared experience? All it can say to them is: "keep out the strangeness! The sole basis of marriage is love, intimacy, and mutual openness." And therefore as time goes on and it becomes harder and harder to keep oneself conformed to what the other expects, as misunderstandings multiply and the hunger for intimacy becomes habitually violated in the marriage bed itself, the couple draws the only conclusion possible, that they are not made for each other, that they are fundamentally unlike each other and strangers ("incompatible" is the popular term), that no basis exists for their married love, i.e., for mutual openness, and therefore that divorce is the only possible step. In other words, this ethic of love *makes divorce inevitable among people who insist on being persons before each other*. Only the hypocrite can stay married.

d. What does such an ethic have to say to the problem of integration? It can only give the fantastic injunction for white and black to become intimately friendly and to dismiss (by magic?) the dismay of strangeness one feels before the other.

e. What does it say to parents and children, who, as the children grow up and become themselves full-fledged persons and strangers, must give up the relation of intimacy and learn to live with each other as adult strangers? It has nothing to say at all, except the impossible—and for the children humiliating—injunction to go on in intimacy, as if there were no growing up at all.

3. Worse perhaps than its own inability to face these real problems, this ethic has deprived people of their *consciousness* of this feeling of strangeness and has made them unable to grapple with it. It has created a mindset which can see ethical problems only in the personal terms, only in relation to personal friends and personal enemies. In

most people, the feeling of strangeness is left without even the most basic level of guidance, that of self-consciousness. People do not know that this is one of their chief torments. They think that their dismay before a policeman has something to do with their lack of respect for the law or with their fear of a fine! People have no familiar name for this feeling. They do not recognize either its existence or its power.

4. Finally, can you imagine what this notion of love as intimate mutual understanding, as the exclusion of strangeness, does to the love which man should have for God? God has to become someone we can understand. No Trinity! No wrath! No impenetrable mystery of election! No sir! [McGill has written in the margin: "Fear and Trembling."] God must have our values, our visions, our dullness. Otherwise, if he confronts us as mystery and holiness it would be impossible to "love" him.

This is the substance of my criticism of your approach. My own reading of Christian love is that it calls us, not to enjoy each other in familiarity, but to affirm each other in strangeness. It is in *this* connection that I understand the kind of qualities which the New Testament associates with love: patience, forgiveness, no judgment, etc. The ethic of Jesus, then, is significant, not because it removes our mutual strangeness, but because it gives us a context in which to affirm and rejoice in that strangeness as something true and good.[5] It even teaches us to accept our strangeness to ourselves.

God defines power, not power God.[6]

The issue is the style of the Christian life. God is not a milk bottle for infants. God is a fire. To approach him is to be destroyed in our old way.[7]

Appendix

Theology as Entertainment. Entertainment is not pejorative. Theology is a medium for something other than theology: surprise and the personal. Not *play!*[8] [Theology may be understood as entertainment in] three ways: a. Polemics; b. Take an idea and show how it leads to "unexpected" consequences. "Unexpected" means it challenges, revises or inverts familiar ways

---

5. See Abner Dean, "Grace Note," Introduction, 11.

6. From folder #110: "Theology 101—Notes."

7. From folder #97: "Death in Baptism and Eucharist: Notes."

8. But there is play, and there is . . . play.

of understanding; c. Take an idea and build a whole universe. The scope is fascinating. Karl Barth developed this more than anyone.[9]

[In the context of notes on baptism: This is] not narrow. [This is] not [to] ignore other religions. On the contrary, one of my main concerns is to indicate the terms for *engaging* men who do not believe—whether [of] other religions, or whatever. All interpretational claims are too tortuous—arguments about what we believe and others believe. Intellectual apologetics misconceives the arena. But baptism points differently: to the reality of dying. And this is the point where men are addressed, men of other faiths. Not Western Christianity and not Vatican Catholicism: but let go identity. [This dying is] radical enough to touch at a point beneath cultural self-investments.[10]

[The following remarks are transcribed from a recording of a lecture, "Against the Rich Man's Gospel," given at St. John's University, Collegeville, Minnesota, Summer, 1970.]

Questioner: Doctor, it's disturbing the way you put it. And the question is, do you think that it's possible for many individuals to come to that ideal?

McGill: I would assume that deep down I suppose most individuals come to this idea about the bankruptcy of having by the age of thirty. The forms of possessive life keep going, and they maintain those forms. But they no longer believe in them. So that, no, I don't think this is any rare, esoteric insight at all.

Questioner: . . . [I]s it possible for us to come up to that ideal and live that way . . . ? Not from where you attack the idea of the philosophy of possession . . .

McGill: Well, I would have to say, first of all, that normally this would not be possible apart from a community where this kind of style of life, this sense of life, flourishes. I don't—you know, it's possible for an individual to do this on his own, but that would be extraordinarily rare. No, normally . . . what you're really asking then [is] are there communities where flowing life rather than possessed life becomes a more normal sense of things? Well, on the one hand, I don't think *any* community, including the church, lives this way without distortions, falsifications, and betrayals. But on the other hand, [in] the church, and also not only [in] the church but [in] some

9. From a folder labeled "Appendix: Theology" (file #404).

10. From folder #97—"Death in Baptism and Eucharist: Notes."

natural forms of life, this component often occurs. The point where in the natural forms of life the flowing style, the letting-go style, gets complicated is at the horizon of death. But, nevertheless, looking at other cultures than western European culture, one is very impressed with—what one might say—the question of having is not as absolute as certainly our [Western] world would make it seem. So I just have to leave it open and say I don't think it's an ideal at all. But on the other hand, the kind of consistent execution of it is probably always being [fallen?] down. Nor do I believe that it is only in the name of Jesus that it happens. It seems to me this is an element in the natural forms of life. The question of death, though, becomes very critical. Of course, the question of death . . . for me having is the meaning of sin. On the side in relation to God, to have is no longer to need to receive. On the relation of the neighbor, to have is to not give. So I would analyze the seven deadly sins as modes of authorizing having or of emotions associated with the desire for having. And therefore, in this regard, the doctrine of the Trinity where the Father gives all to the Son, the Son returns all to the Father in the unity of the Spirit, is the abolition of having from the very being of God. Now there are doctrines of God and there are theological doctrines of man which authorize having and which make it seem that God's divinity consists in having something. And that interprets the resurrection as men getting something and having something. Therefore, this would be a very classic case of what I would consider the triumph of sin in Christian theology. And this is always going on. And certainly the whole notion of reward and punishment is to elevate the gospel of having[11] into sort of absolute proportions. But the techniques in which the having enters certainly into the Christian consciousness are fascinating to watch, and the church is always fighting at one front to finding them creeping up on another front. And the church fights material possessions; and before you know it, there's a whole cult of spiritual possessiveness, when the church fights possessiveness on the part of men and gets a doctrine of God as having everything and men as having nothing and you get this Calvinistic dreadful thing where God is everything and man is empty in contrast. So that the clear difficulty of not being deceived by possession pervades the whole history of the Christian community and represents part of the living edge of its history. The American experience is a most interesting one in this regard, and Father Gallen,[12] of course, can speak a great deal of that.

11. See ch. VI, 107, n. 2.

12. Father John Gallen, SJ, was on the summer school faculty at St. John's University,

Questioner: . . . [W]hy don't more communities spring up . . . ?

McGill: Well, I suppose I would put the problem at a different point and, by shifting it, may[be] change the urgency of it. The question isn't do you take. Of course you take. The question is: Is the energy of your life in letting go and the relaxed moments in taking? Or is the energy in life in seizing and the relaxed moments in letting go? I have to get really psychologically realistic. One would have to recognize that the rather pivotal question is where one has a sense of one's vitality. And one might really take D. H. Lawrence's argument and say, well, any sense of the vitality of life is always in the communication of life, never in the having,[13] and that the very gospel of having is itself an expression of despair. This is to take the position that experience really teaches us the true and that having is really a kind of despair, a kind of really growing out of and a kind of dreadful despair of all things. Now the question why—why is the energy of having and the cult of possession and the sense of coping with every evil by anticipating it

---

Collegeville, Minnesota, from 1968 to 1974. He founded the North American Academy of Liturgy in 1973, was elected NAAL's first president in 1975, and received the Academy's Berakah Award in 2000.

13. In his lecture, McGill quotes Lawrence's poem, "We are Transmitters":

As we live, we are transmitters of life.
And when we fail to transmit life, life fails to flow through us.

This is part of the mystery of sex, it is a flow onwards.
Sexless people transmit nothing.

And if, as we work, we can transmit life into our work,
life, still more life, rushes into us to compensate, to be ready
and we ripple with life through the days.

Even if it is a woman making an apple dumpling, or a man a stool,
if life goes into the pudding, good is the pudding
good is the stool,
content is the woman, with fresh life rippling in to her,
content is the man.

Give, and it shall be given unto you
is still the truth about life.
But giving life is not so easy.
It doesn't mean handing it out to some mean fool, or letting the living dead eat you up.
It means kindling the life-quality where it was not,
even if it's only in the whiteness of a washed pocket-handkerchief.

"We Are Transmitters" in eds. Vivian de Sola Pinto and Warren Roberts, *The Complete Poems of D. H. Lawrence* (New York: Viking, 1964), I, 449. D. H. Lawrence lived from 1885 to 1930.

and securing some possession ahead of time—why is this so strong when it doesn't take much life to know it's false? Well, I mean, are we not getting very close to the meaning of evil? I mean the real meaning of evil is precisely to find yourself trapped in that which you don't believe in.[14] I mean if evil were all a matter of self-conscious error or deliberate choice, well, then, we could always undo our evils. No, there's something insidious about this, strangely insidious; and the patristic church was particularly aware [of this], at the moment when it ceased to be an underground church that was persecuted and became first a legal religion and finally the official religion of the Roman Empire, so anyone seeking a government position anywhere had to be a baptized Christian. Suddenly this insidiousness of possession, the insidiousness of having, was recognized; and all kinds of techniques were developed to try to counteract it. Now why is it that this untruth has such momentum, such incredible power? It almost works on its own, you know. And at one level, I suppose most people know it's empty; it really doesn't get you anything. And it goes on and on and on and gathers such terrific energy. Well, I suppose what I'm saying in expressing this way is my conviction that evil is demonic and not human; and if we find ourselves caught up in this false way of life, we are caught up into it not because *we* give it power and *we* will to live with it, but because it seems to have a power of its own that holds us and gathers us up even if we don't like it, even if we want to go against it. And really I don't think much advance can be made on problems of this level until the church is willing to let go of its moralistic conception of evil and is more willing to pick up a demonic sense of evil.

Questioner: And how it is that Jesus is not breaking into more lives . . .?

McGill: Well, you know, there's a very old answer to that. When the name of Jesus is invoked for evil, Jesus—the power of Jesus—withdraws. That is to say, if the name of Jesus gets entangled with perverse and corrupt forms, then it's God's mercy to discredit the power associated with Jesus in parenthesis. I mean this whole notion of prophetic judgment, of God's chastisement, of the silence of God before those who abusively misuse and overuse his name, is something so common in the history of the old Israel and new Israel. No . . . I mean if people are exploiting Jesus, if people are using the power of Jesus in all kinds of corrupt ways, if Jesus is secularized and completely domesticated, then it is our hope that the power of Jesus will disappear for awhile so it can be the one it is. No, I'm

14. See *Sermons of Arthur C. McGill*, 1, 58–59.

not really convinced that the power of God depends on constantly sort of proving himself Madison Avenue-wise. Lux soap must do this, but I'm not sure Jesus must. We are taught to think, if everybody isn't running after him, if the churches aren't full, oh gee-wiz. But you know it's much more subtle than that. And one isn't sure with people. It's always my surprise that sometimes the ones most apparently self-secure, where, one might say, the · godless self-sufficiency is most visually presented and most systematically disclosed in every corner of their lives, may turn out to be the ones which inside themselves are most contemptuous of this. So I have more and more difficulty summing up the United States as *Time* magazine does every week. I sense these difficulties, but I'm not sure that I would identify the presence or absence of God with my perception of the presence or absence of God. And since God works invisibly as well as visibly, I really don't finally say that the absence of God in the order of visibility is really the absence of God working. So the fact that people leave the church and the fact that the church becomes poor makes it a purer vessel of its Lord. And therefore when the church becomes rich, when Israel becomes rich, and you have your summer houses, you cows of Bashan [see Amos 4:1],[15] why in comes Nebuchadnezzar.[16] No, I mean . . . I don't know what to say. Obviously, I think we're coming to a time when Christianity is going to be not the center of life at all. It's going to be underground or at least a quite peripheral institution. And Christians who identify God with power and having and wealth are going to think that the disappearance of Christianity from the center of western civilization is due to God's discredit. But it seems to me this is a moment of great spiritual clarification. And perhaps we will get poorer before we get richer.

15. McGill is surely referring to Amos' "cows of Bashan," though the recording sounds clearly like "Shian": "Bashan [fruitful, stoneless plain] . . . The greater part of Bashan consisted of a tableland which ranges from 1,600 to 2,300 feet in height. It was well adapted for wheat growing and cattle raising, and was famous for its groves of oak trees. These natural features appear often in the poetry of the Bible. The strong bulls of Bashan typify the fierce enemies that beset the righteous man (Ps. 22:12); the luxurious, pleasure-seeking women of Samaria are 'cows of Bashan' (Amos 4:1)"—Simon Cohen, "Bashan," in ed. George Arthur Buttrick, *The Interpreter's Dictionary of the Bible* (Nashville: Abingdon, 1962), vol. 1, 363.

16. Nebuchadnezzar II (or Nebuchadrezzar) was king of Babylonia, 605–562 B.C.E. McGill is alluding to the razing of Jerusalem and the burning of the temple under Nebuchadnezzar in 587 B.C.E., beginning the Babylonian Exile, 587–538 B.C.E. See Jeremiah 21–52.

Appendix

Arthur McGill's Harvard Divinity School Courses, 1970–1980

Theology 101. Recent Theological Writings (Taught with Professor Gordon Kaufman)

An examination of developments in Christian theology in the twentieth century.

Theology 146. The Knowledge of God

A study of the role of symbol and myth in the Christian knowledge of God. This course will review the terms on which natural science and the theology of the last three centuries have rejected these as modes of knowledge and will examine their recent rehabilitation.

Theology 161. The Reality of Jesus   To be offered in 1974–75
                                            To be offered in 1975–76
                                            To be offered in 1976–77
                                            To be offered in 1978–79

A review of the Protestant effort to find the "real" Jesus by means of historical investigation; an examination of the reaction of recent theologians to the failure of this effort, with their recourse to such categories as miracle (Barth), myth (Altizer) and eschatology (Bultmann); and a survey of the impact of this crisis on Christian worship and morals.

Theology 161. The Reality of Jesus   To be offered 1980–81

An examination of the various ways in which Jesus has been considered "real," ranging from an emphasis on his impact on people's personal experience or on his historical existence, to a preoccupation with his sacramental efficacy or with his bringing an eschatological hope.

Theology 163. Impoverishment

To be offered 1974–75
To be offered 1976–77

The course will (1) consider several different types of actual impoverishment in detail, drawing especially on the work of students in field education projects; (2) examine values with which American society interprets poverty and the ways in which people are educated—and may be re-educated regarding these values; (3) study certain aspects of New Testament Christology which bear on the meaning and conquest of poverty.

Theology 164. Religion and Culture: T. S. Eliot

Eliot's work—poetic, dramatic, and critical—will be taken as the basis for the consideration of four themes: (1) the mystical and eschatological aspects of Christian existence (the saint); (2) culture as the formation and fruit of Christian life (education); (3) the significance of literature in relation to culture and Christian faith (the writer); (4) alienation and the decay of Western civilization (contemporary history).

Theology 165.
Death and the Death of Jesus Christ

To be offered in 1977–78
To be offered in 1979–80

An examination of the death of Jesus Christ in terms of several biblical and contemporary images by which the character of death is actualized; in terms of the notions of God, of Jesus Christ and of life which are entailed in each of these images; and in terms of the ways in which these images discourage people from, or liberate them for, dying and letting others die.

Theology 165. Death and the Death of Jesus Christ

This course will review the different images used in Paul's letters on the one hand and in John's Gospel on the other, to actualize the character of Jesus' death. It will then examine the very different image of death as a "catastrophic mutilation" that dominates contemporary experience.

Theology 168. History of Christian Theology in the Twentieth Century

This course will survey both the critical and constructive efforts of Christian theology from 1920 to the present in both the Protestant and Roman Catholic churches.

Theology 227. Seminar on a Theological Problem

The conflicts between a Pauline and a Johanine theology: an approach to the problem of authority and diversity.

Theology 227. Seminar on a Theological Problem

> The problem of love.

Theology 230. Seminar: Karl Barth　　　To be offered in 1976–77
　　　　　　　　　　　　　　　　　　　To be offered in 1978–79

The atheism represented by Ludwig Feuerbach, and the attempt of Karl Barth both to acknowledge and to circumvent that atheism.

Theology 232. Seminar: Studies in Historical Theology

A study of the major theological controversies.

Theology 232.
Seminar: Contemporary Theology　　　To be offered spring 1977–78

Readings in liberation theology.

Theology 232.
Seminar: Contemporary Theology　　　To be offered in 1979–80

Readings in recent theologians.

Theology 233. Seminar: Medieval Theology

An examination of the theology and piety of Anselm of Canterbury.

Theology 226. Seminar: Studies in Theological Method—Phenomenology

To be offered in 1976–77

An examination of the bearing of phenomenology on theological inquiry. This will involve a study of several kinds of phenomenology (Husserl, Heidegger, and Merleau-Ponty) and efforts to develop a phenomenology of religion.

Theology 226. Seminar: Studies in Theological Method: Phenomenology

To be offered in 1977–78

An examination of the bearing of phenomenology on theological inquiry. This seminar will concentrate on Husserl's description of human knowledge, and on developments made from this description by others (e.g., Merleau-Ponty, Alfred Schutz, Paul Ricoeur).

Theology 300. Colloquium   (Taught with Professor George Rupp)

A seminar given in conjunction with Theology 102. This is normally required of all Th.M. candidates and of all Th.D. and Ph.D. candidates who are preparing for general examinations.